Sounds of Joy

We have always had great respect for Dora who raised four wonderful boys and ran a business of her own. She did not consider herself handicapped. It was a marvelous time to see her after she had regained her hearing. We cried from happiness then and when we spoke with her by telephone a short while later. Herbert remembers well the time, 20 years ago, when he called her and she could not hear him. It is truly a miracle and we are happy to know that she is sharing her story and using her hearing in the way that God wants.

Herbert and Lila Tingelstad
Brother and Sis-in-law

I remember Dora very well. I was very impressed with her "spirit" and courage and I am so pleased that she had a successful cochlear implant. I am also pleased that she has written about her wonderful experiences. It is an excellent book. I love the design and admire her style.

Thomas J. McDonald, M.D.
Professor and Chairman
Dept. of Otorhinotaryngology
Mayo Clinic, Rochester, Minn.

I met Dora when I began going to craft sales with my parents when I was three years old. My mom always told me, "Look at Dora when you speak to her because she can't hear and has to read your lips."

As I grew older, I spoke faster and it was difficult for Dora to understand me. We resorted to writing notes on napkins and scraps of paper. I was so happy to hear that she had regained her hearing. I was the first person she spoke with on the telephone. Dora has made me a better person as I learned to respect and understand people with disabilities. She wasn't any different than you or I. The only thing she couldn't do was hear. Now she can do that.

Tanya Frank
Student, Univ. of North Dakota
Grand Forks, N.D.

Your book is wonderful. It is always nice to hear from satisfied implant users. It is especially rewarding to us working at Cochlear to know what a positive impact cochlear implants have. We are thankful to you, too, for being such a wonderful advocate for Cochlear Corporation and cochlear implants. It is people like you who make coming to work a pleasure.

Glenda Harper
Sr. Marketing Clerk
Cochlear Corporation

I do not remember you as being hearing impaired. I don't recall my parents ever pointing out people's differences, which left me naive about many things but encouraged me to relate to people for what they are inside. By coincidence, I do much television production for the Medical Center at the University of California, San Francisco. A video I produced there was of a young woman who received one of the first Clarion implants. Overnight, I became familiar with the miracles of cochlear implants. I can still see the marvel on that woman's face when she described what she was hearing. I am so happy that you had the same good fortune.

Ian (Jim) Pearson
Pearson Communications
Tiburon, Calif.

I am so happy to hear of the wonderful ways that God works in your life. Many blessings to you. Praise God for the miracle of life, health, medical science, and open ears.

Pastor Robert Mrosko
St. Mark Lutheran Church
Ruskin, Neb.

I never knew, during the twelve years that Dora and I were classmates, that she had a hearing impairment which eventually left her deaf. Now I've witnessed her miracle, her re-awakening. She doesn't hesitate to share her enthusiasm and appreciation for life's offerings. I love it when she says she can hear Johnny Cash, the singing of the birds, and the voices of her grandchildren. Here comes Dora! She's an inspiration to me and a good friend. She could have titled her book *Journey Into Our World* and we're richer because she's "hear" with us.

Ardis (Sanden) Nelson

Classmate

Journey Out of Silence is far more than a story about Dora Weber's life and healing. It is a testimony of God's blessings upon us all. It is a reminder that God answers prayers in His way and in His time. It is an example of God using all people to work toward his purpose. Some may say that Dora's hearing is a result of scientific advancements in technology. But even the world of science and technology belong to God. He desired Dora's heart and soul even more than He desired her to hear again. It is obvious from this book that God's desire for Dora has been fulfilled. We should be thrilled with this miracle of Dora's restored hearing, as were those people who were directly healed by Jesus during his life on earth. It is even more exciting to hear the story of Dora's journey to a closer walk with her Lord. This journey promises to bring her eternal joy. This journey promises to be a continued blessing and testimony to others. This journey is eternal. Thank you, Dora.

Timothy L. Tingelstad (nephew)

Attorney-at-law

Bemidji, Minn.

I was so surprised and happy to hear from my dear former pupil, Dora. I am so happy that you have your hearing back. Ears are so delicate and hearing so important to one's life.

I am 90 years old and very healthy and get along fine with the hearing aids that I wear. I have for the past 20 years been a "Bingo caller" at the Emmanuel Community Nursing Home in Detroit Lakes. I believe that God created us for a purpose and that he is pleased when we forget ourselves and strive to help others

Evelyn Nicholson McCanna

2nd Grade Teacher

Journey Out of Silence

Dora Tingelstad Weber

Foreword by
Samuel C. Levine, M.D., FACS
Associate Professor
Dept. of Otolaryngology

Front cover design by Scott M. Weber

Graphic and Photo of Nucleus Spectra 22 Compliments of
    Cochlear Corporation
    61 Inverness Drive East
    Suite 200
    Englewood, Colo. 80112
        Telephone 1-303-790-9010
        Hotline Numbers: 800-458-4999
        Voice 800-483-3123 TTY

Quotes from Heartland Samplers
Used with permission of
    Heartland Samplers Inc.
    3255 Spring St. NE
    Minneapolis, Minn. 55413

ISBN 1-890676-30-6

Library of Congress Catalog Number: 98-88500

Printed in the United States of America.

J   I   H   G   F   E   D   C   B A

Beaver's Pond Press, Inc.

5125 Danen's Drive
Edina, Minnesota 55439-1465

OTHER PUBLISHED WORKS —DORA WEBER

Lumberjack's Music Brought Pair Together—essay
    Published in *We Made our Own Fun* by Reminisce Books

It's Spring—The Meadow's Reborn
    A Question of Balance—National Library of Poetry

Trees
    Best Poems of 1996—National Library of Poetry

Town of Heaven—State of Hope
    Distinguished Poets of America—National Library of Poetry

Yesterday's Tomorrow—
    Poetic Voices of America, Spring 1993
    Sparrow Grass Poetry, Forum, Inc.

Dedicated in the hope
that all may hear
to
Dr. Samuel C. Levine
and
Sharon Smith, M.S., CCC-A

With love and thankfulness
to
Pastor Gary Galchutt
Jeffery, Justin, Jacob,
Chelsea, Brandon
and all future
grandchildren

CONTENTS

Dedication v
God's Gift to Dora xi
Foreword xv
Preface xix
In Memory xxi
Introduction xxiii
Acknowledgments xxv

PART ONE
   Down in the Valley...1
   Getting to Know You 6
   Let's Play Pretend 9
   Wind in the Willows 13
   A Knot Around My Neck...............................17
   We Regret to Inform You...............................20

PART TWO
   Star Light—Star Bright 29
   In Victory There Was Sorrow 35
   Precious Memories 37
   It's All in My Head 40
   A Penny for Your Thoughts............................42
   Please, God, Not Me, Too...............................48

PART THREE
   True Grit 53
   Rain on the Roof..58
   A Secret No More 59
   I Want to Go With You 61
   Enduring Courage 62
   Against All Odds...66

Part Four

Guiding Light 75

To Know Them Was to Love Them 78

First Love—A Tribute to Bill.............................82

Etched on Stone 84

Restless Moments 88

Only a Dream...90

Lonesome Once More.......................................92

No Improvement 96

The Unveiling...99

Part Five

I'll Love Him Forever 103

I Pledge Thee My Tross 107

And Baby Makes Three....................................111

Bad News...114

Warning Signs...116

I Didn't Want to Go...117

A Knock on the Door 120

Part Six

Just a Matter of Time 125

I Don't Want to be a Burden..............................130

I Can, Too, Still Hear 132

Stop the World and Let Me Off...........................135

They Gave to Me...137

That's Okay—That's All Right 141

No, Doctor, You Must Be Mistaken......................143

Part Seven

Blowing in the Wind..147

McDonald's Angels 150

God Isn't Finished With Me Yet..........................153

I Just Look That Way 157

Show Grandma What You Want..........................162

PART EIGHT

Leap of Faith 167

The Pink Pig 169

God Meets with the Angels 173

I Want to Hear My Grandsons Speak 174

A Sound Decision 176

The Lions' Touch 179

Last Resort 182

Waiting and Praying 184

Whatever Will Be 187

Ephphatha 189

Touched by an Angel 191

Let Go—Let God 194

It Will Work 198

PART NINE

Beyond the Silence 205

Blessed Assurance 209

Outside the Soundproof Booth 212

Silent No More 214

Can She Hear the Birds 217

Gramma Can Hear Me Now! 220

Oh, Give Me a Home 221

Shout of Acclamation 223

Hold the Line 224

In the Garden 227

PART TEN

Recollections—Reflections—Resurrection 229

Afterword 249

Glossary 257

About the Author 261

GOD'S GIFT TO DORA

I was called to serve as pastor of Prince of Peace Lutheran Church, Spring Lake Park, Minn. in January 1986. I came to know the officers and their families very quickly. Dora's husband, Myron, served as the congregational secretary at Council and Voters Meetings.

When I met Dora, she seemed to be completely accepting of her disability, that of deafness. Dora was very easy about speaking and getting notes in return. When I came to visit, the writing tablet was out so that I could jot down notes, questions, and remarks. Her humor and laughter were very appropriate. The warmth of her family, her husband and four sons, surrounded my visits and Dora shared in a confident and natural manner. This was also true at church, with neighbors and at her coffee stop, the McDonald's restaurant in Spring Lake Park.

However, after a few years the family expanded. I officiated at the wedding of Dora and Myron's oldest son. This introduced a daughter-in-law. In a few years, there was a grandson. As the grandson started speaking his first words, I heard Dora say, "I cannot hear my own grandson."

She told of her fond love of the years when her four sons were speaking their first words. She told of how she helped her sons learn new words. More than the daughters-in-law, it was the grandchildren who created this great longing in Dora to re-enter the world of sound. It was hard to see the longing and yearning grow because it was so very maternal, so very spontaneous, so natural for any woman.

A few years after that, Dora shared with me a procedure called the cochlear implant and how the deaf were being helped to regain their hearing. She did not yet fully understand the details but she did know that she and Myron would investigate further. We all agreed that the Lord would lead them as they began their search and they requested prayer. If the interest within them grew, that would be under the Lord's blessing.

As a pastor, I know of very few ventures so guided by prayer and the Lord's leading from beginning to end.

Along with the first contacts at the University of Minnesota Hospital, Dora and Myron made a trip one weekend on which Dora experienced many sensations and feelings in and about one ear. They were strong and seemed almost as if the Lord was touching her. It seemed odd that this was happening with the ear that had been without hearing the longest and on which four previous ear surgeries had failed. Was it not amazing, then, that in the actual implant surgery, it was this ear that was chosen over the ear that heard last?

Meanwhile, it became clearer that the Lord was leading and blessing every appointment. Dora needed to be approved in so many tests, questioning sessions and medical exams. It was becoming a real wonder that nothing became an insurmountable barrier on Dora's path to surgery. In her own mind, she was content to go on even though it was wearisome and without a guarantee that her hearing would be restored.

About this time, Dora came for a spiritual visit with me, her pastor, relating a very special assurance she received. It happened when she stopped at McDonald's Restaurant for coffee after one of her morning walks. It was 6:30 a.m. and she was the only customer in the restaurant. Was it not strange, then, that at that time of Dora's pensive waiting, a man came in who already had a successful cochlear implant and sat in the booth right in front of her? How could it be that this successfully recovered patient was in this McDonald's Restaurant at this particular time to find another deaf person who wanted the surgery?

It seemed so strange and marvelous in its timing that Dora felt and experienced strong reassurance from this morning conversation at the restaurant. It was almost like an angel's visit.

As Dora went forward, her pastor and congregation prayed for her every week. It was an uncertain journey because while the doctor and audiologist were very optimistic, they could only give her general answers about the developments ahead because each patient is different.

Waiting on the doctor and the surgery was a path of patience with spiritual overtones. In Dora's congregation, the conviction was growing that Dora was being led to success by the Lord. No matter how narrow the chances were for Dora to go on, she passed all tests with flying colors.

Her pastor, friends, and church began praying with quiet confidence. The Lord was going to bless the rest of the procedure, guiding the doctor, helping Dora with faith and peace. Now it was going to be step by step for Dora toward receiving the gift of hearing.

Many around Dora were waiting on the Lord for the day of surgery. The operation went well but it would be weeks before she would know the outcome. The doctor and audiologist were very encouraging. When the day of hookup arrived, Dora was delighted at the first sounds she heard. In the end, success was so complete that Dora's full recovery of the shades of sound and the variety of voices has placed her as one of the University of Minnesota's most successful patients to regain hearing.

Naturally, Dora's church had special prayers of thanksgiving for Dora's recovery of hearing. The pastor and members were mindful of how many contributed to her medical care during this procedure. Their keen minds and education were all part of Dora's path to success. Yet, because of the initial leading of the Lord, Dora was able to overcome the many hurdles and the pastor led her church family in thanks and praise for *God's gift to Dora.*

We gave warm and hearty thanks that now the little grandchildren could speak to their grandma. How beautiful the gifts of the Lord! Every word, every sigh and sound of each precious grandchild was heard by Dora now in the great break through of this medical miracle to restore hearing.

Dora shows and keeps her thanks to God alive by sharing her story as often as she can. She speaks at women's church groups and at various Lions International functions whenever she has the opportunity. She now hopes there will be interest in her written story of *God's gift to her*—to hear again.

Pastor Gary Galchutt
Pastor of Prince of Peace Lutheran Church (retired)
Spring Lake Park, Minn.

Pastor Gary Galchutt and Jeffery

FOREWORD

I appreciate the opportunity to write the Foreword to *Journey Out of Silence*.

My interest in hearing loss is closely personal. My uncle (my father's brother) lost his hearing during the second World War. He contracted a jungle fever in the Asian Theater of the war and came home with a hearing loss. During most of my childhood, my uncle continued to use hearing aids rather poorly. He found it increasingly difficult to communicate and he found himself to be more and more isolated. This was a sharp contrast to his nature which was extremely outgoing. I gather that when he was younger, he was quite active and was the life of the party. According to my father, he spent most of his youth as the life of the party. By the time that I really remember him, we had trouble communicating. I remember that his son tended to take advantage of the fact that his father could not really hear. Over the years it became obvious to the members of the family that his problem was getting worse and was very

Samuel Levine, M.D., F.A.C.S.

destructive to his personal relationships, his work, and his enjoyment of life.

When I left home and went to Northwestern University, I studied engineering and I had an interest in biomedical studies. I worked in an artificial lung laboratory. One of the courses that I was required to take was offered by a famous ear researcher. This was a difficult class and required a project to finish it for credit. I decided to attempt a mathematical model of cochlear function based on a mechanical analog instead of an electrical one. The project turned out to be much harder than I thought at the time. My interest in otology waned after that experience.

I again became interested in ear research and studies in medical school when I learned that I was not physically strong enough to become an orthopedic surgeon. I was allowed to do a lot of research in orthopedics and got a really good experience. Unfortunately, I knew that my career was not headed in that direction. I finally decided to try another area of surgery and really stumbled upon ear surgery. An internship is a miserable experience and mine was exceptionally miserable. When I started otolaryngology, I went to the dissection laboratory for my first experience. I had wonderful teachers and in a short period of time (like two weeks), I decided that my future had finally taken form. For me it was like emerging from a long dark tunnel into the sunlight. I came home to my wife and with great excitement described what I planned to do with my life. My wife now describes this as a burning bush experience. You may recall from your biblical reading that God came to Moses in the desert, speaking to him through a bush which was on fire but was not consumed. At the time, I believe that my wife thought that I had lost my mind. Somehow that evening when all my previous experience came together, I was able to chart my own course.

After a short six year study period, I began as a very young assistant professor in the department. At the time, the department was considering starting a cochlear implant program and I was lucky enough to be part of this program. I spoke with my uncle at a family party and tried to convince him to consider a cochlear implant. He went to New York and saw one of the experts about this. His wife called me several days later and told me that he had decided that he would have the implant but he planned to come to Minnesota so that I would do it. I had severe misgivings. What if something went wrong? After discussion with several other doctors in the field, we decided to go ahead. The procedure went well and has made a tremendous difference in his life. My feelings about the implant couldn't be stronger. My first hand experience tells me that this is a dramatic difference and influence in someone's life. It is for me a mission, and a personal pleasure to be able to participate in the cochlear implant process.

Respectfully,

Sam Levine, M.D., FACS
Associate Professor
Department of Otolaryngology
University of Minnesota

PREFACE

My first real awareness of cochlear implants came while I was a doctoral student at the University of Virginia, in the early 1980s. A fellow graduate student was working with several implant patients as part of her Ph.D. thesis, and I frequently observed parts of the research sessions.

Nearly all of the patients relied heavily on signing or lip reading to supplement the auditory input provided by their implants. Implants did restore some level of hearing to these listeners, but they were crude devices by today's standards, and they certainly did not allow listeners to approach normal communication function even under ideal circumstances. Cochlear implants were unusual, experimental devices, and their future was still uncertain.

In 1994, I accepted a position working with Dr. David Nelson in the Clinical Psychoacoustics Laboratory at the University of Minnesota. I was given responsibility for overseeing the day to day operations of the cochlear implant research program, and given the freedom to develop new areas of research related to hearing perception in cochlear implant listeners. My entry into cochlear implant research occurred at an exciting time, just as a new generation of speech processing strategies was coming to market, allowing many cochlear implant listeners to achieve unprecedented levels of speech recognition performance with their prostheses.

One of the primary goals of our work in the Clinical Psychoacoustics Lab is to understand speech recognition in implant listeners. Why are many listeners doing so much better with the newer speech processors? Why are some still doing so poorly? Can speech recognition performance be understood on the basis of psychoacoustic abilities? How do electrical stimulus parameters affect psychoacoustic abilities and speech recognition? What happens to speech recognition in background noise?

A number of cochlear implant listeners are helping us to address these questions by participating in psychoacoustic and speech recognition experiments. Currently we are working with individuals who have the Cochlear Corporation Nucleus 22 prosthesis or the Advanced Bionics Clarion device.

We are fortunate to have a superb group of dedicated and enthusiastic implant subjects who are willing to attend regular research sessions—sometimes as frequently as 2-3 times per week over the course of months or years. This allows us to obtain detailed information on hearing perception in individual subjects, information that we believe will translate into additional improvements in later generations of implant devices.

Dora Weber has been an active research subject in our laboratory since November, 1996, shortly after she first received her Nucleus 22 implant. She is a true champion of our cause, an enthusiastic and hard-working subject, and a delightful person. She is also very communicative, a great talker and an equally great listener. Knowing Dora as I do now, it is hard to imagine that she was deprived of spontaneous oral-aural communication for the many years that she was profoundly deaf. It has been a joy to witness her journey back into the world of hearing and to have some small role in that journey.

Gail Donaldson, Ph.D.
Lions 5M Clinical Psychoacoustics Laboratory
University of Minnesota

In Memory

Lawrence R. Boies, M.A., M.D., was born in Renville, Minn. in 1898. He graduated from the St. Croix Falls High School in 1915 and entered the University of Wisconsin. His studies were interrupted by World War I when he served as a corpsman in the Medical Corps of the U.S. Army.

Returning to the University of Wisconsin, he received his B.A. degree in 1922 and an M.A. degree in 1923 while the first two years of the medical course were being completed.

He taught in the Pipestone, Minn. High School during 1923-24 and then entered the College of Physicians and Surgeons of Columbia University where he received an M.D. degree in 1926. After internship and 19 months of practice as an assistant to a general surgeon in Minneapolis, he enrolled as a graduate student at Harvard Medical School. This period, including a residency at the Massachusetts Eye and Ear Infirmary, covered a period of 25 months.

Doctor Boies married Louise Marty in 1928. They had three sons, Dr. Lawrence R. Boies, Jr., David, a graduate of Yale Law School and William (deceased). He established a private practice in otolaryngology in Minneapolis. Shortly after, in 1931, he was appointed to the University of Minnesota Medical School faculty. In 1955, he became the first full-time head of Otolaryngology. He accomplished a great deal because he was not particularly concerned about credit as long as the work got done.

On Dr. Boies' retirement in 1967, he went on as Executive Director of the Deafness Research Foundation headquartered in New York.

Dr. Lawrence R. Boies passed away July 6, 1986.

Compliments of Dr. Lawrence R. Boies, Jr.

Lawrence R. Boies, M.A., M.D.

INTRODUCTION

When I first began to think about writing *Journey Out of Silence,* I was unsure as to when my travels began. As I thought about it, the clearer it became to me that preparations began the day I was born and continued on until I reached the age of eighteen. By then I had the memories of many sounds that I would not hear again for forty years, packed away in every nook and cranny of my mind.

When I looked back on the roads I traveled after my first stapes mobilization surgery at the University of Minnesota on August 16, 1957, I realized that I had taken many detours before I returned to the road that took me back to where I began. The detours were sometimes over rocky roads and sometimes smooth. I traveled over mountains and I rode the waves of Euphoria.

At times, the road was narrow and I came to several unexpected dead ends. I stopped at rest stops along the way but always traveled on until in 1986. I had grown so weary by then that I just could not go that extra mile. Ten years later, my will to hear my grandsons speak was so great that it got me back on the road. This time I only had to travel six months before I reached my destination. I had come full circle.

My reason for writing *Journey Out of Silence* is personal. I want to share my experiences with everyone—the deaf, the hearing impaired and the hearing. I want my story to reach every ear in hopes that anyone who is living in silence, like I was, will have the opportunity to learn about the cochlear implant and try "just one more time." I did and I found my dream.

ACKNOWLEDGMENTS

How do I begin to thank everyone who traveled with me on my journey or who stood by the side of the road cheering me as I passed by, without the risk of missing someone? Please forgive me if I did.

I thank:

To my wonderful husband, Myron; my sons, Chuck, Ken, Dave and Scott; my daughters-in-law, Sharon, Janine and Allison; my grandchildren, Jeffery, Justin, Jacob Chelsea and Brandon, for giving me a beautiful home. Papa and Mama; my brothers, Milan, LeRoy, Alvin, Herbert and Loyal and their families for their love; my sister, Eleanor, whose journey was even longer than mine.

To my relatives (Webers and Tingelstads), friends (old and new) and neighbors (past and present) for always including me.

To all my teachers, who consciously or unconsciously, helped me graduate.

To Pastor J.B. Jerstad for planting the seed of faith and to Pastor Donald Illian for showing me how to nurture it.

To Mrs. Marion Pearson for jump-starting my journey and to the Pound family for their love and to Bill, for his inspiration.

To George V. Plaster for believing in me and others with disabilities.

To my doctors, Henry Korda; L.W. Morsman; Lawrence R.
Boies, Sr.; George V. Tangen, Jr.; Robert R. Updegraff;
C.M. Kos; Thomas J. McDonald; Thomas A.
Christiansen; and Samuel C. Levine.

To the congregation of Prince of Peace Lutheran Church
for their prayers, love and concern.

To my friends at the Spring Lake Park McDonald's
Restaurant and my crafter friends for their help and
companionship.

Special thanks to the following for making *Journey Out of
Silence* possible.

To the Lions 5M International for their continuing
support of hearing research at the University.

To my editor, Kathy Paulson, for going so many extra
miles.

To Milton Adams, my publisher.

For their assistance, for believing in me and for their
contributions, I thank: Dr. George L. Adams;
Dr. Lawrence R. Boies, Jr.; Dr. Thomas Christiansen;
Gail Donaldson; Tanya Frank; Tanya Grann, Pastor Gary
Galchutt; Glenda Harper; Keith Klein; Dr. Samuel
Levine; Dr. Thomas J. McDonald; Pastor Robert Mrosko;
Robert Nemeth; Anne Gerber Pearson; Ian Pearson;
Virginia Plaster; Carolyn Rask; Louise Rosendahl;
Sharon Smith; Herbert and Lila Tingelstad; Tim and
Annette Tingelstad, Scott Weber.

A very special thanks to my travel agent, my Lord and Savior
Jesus Christ.

For everything there is a season and a time for every matter under Heaven
A time to weep, and a time to laugh
A time to mourn, and a time to dance
Ecclesiastes 3:1-8

and now an experience of sharing—

PART ONE

DOWN IN THE VALLEY

Stories that Mama told me of my birth and early childhood and the sights and sounds of adolescence are so finely engraved in my mind that with little effort I can regress to those years. Back then when I was carefree, confident and lighthearted. Back then when I could hear.

The excursion is the same when you go looking for your sorrow as when you go looking for your joy.

Eudora Welty

I was born at 3:10 the morning of August 30, 1938 at Boysen Hospital in Pelican Rapids, Minnesota. Mama probably knew I would be a girl. Only my sister, who is five years older, was born in a hospital. My five brothers, age three to sixteen, were born at home.

Papa didn't know how to drive, possibly due to his deafness, so the driving was left to my brother, Milan. Only a few days earlier, when he turned sixteen, he got his driver's license and then had the responsibility to get Mama safely into town before I arrived.

I came close to being born on the sidewalk in front of the hospital so I imagine it to have been a frantic ride in the darkness of night. It must have been quite a relief when they saw the lights of the hospital and the car came to a stop, with a jerk, out in front.

Later that morning, as I laid in Mama's arms, she told me that I was a beautiful little baby. I believed her until I heard the nurses talking about me. Then I had my doubts. How could a ten-pound baby with red hair be little and beautiful?

But later, when Papa brought my brothers, Milan, LeRoy, Alvin, Herbert and Loyal and my sister Eleanor to visit me, I felt better when I saw how good looking they all were. I thought, *Hey, I must be okay after all!*

They were all dressed so nice. Eleanor wore a pretty blue flowered print dress and Papa and the boys were neatly dressed in bib overalls and flannel shirts. When they turned to leave for home, I saw what would become a familiar sight, the red bandanna handkerchief that was hanging out of Papa's back pocket.

I knew that Eleanor would be happy to have a sister and I didn't anticipate Loyal giving me any problems but I wondered about my four older brothers. How would they like having another kid, and a girl at that, tagging along after them? I couldn't wait to get home to find out.

It had begun to rain during the night and it was still raining the next day when Milan came to take Mama and me home. The ungraded roads were very muddy and washed out and when we reached our driveway at the top of the hill, the car became mired in the mud. Mama was still too weak so Milan took me in his arms and carried me down the hill to home.

Home was a forty-acre farm, nestled in a valley, about forty miles southeast of Fargo, N.D. Unlike the shacks that my family had lived in for sixteen years, the little house that I was brought home to was newly built. Mama must have felt like a princess when they moved in and Papa, I'm sure, was happy to finally have a place to call his own even though it wasn't very big.

Much of the land was covered with trees or littered with rocks so it was impossible for Papa to raise enough crops to feed a lot of cattle. He only had three cows, Bessie, Beauty and Blacky and two horses, Doc and Florry. Doc was a big white workhorse and Florry, the one Alvin rescued before she became food for the mink on a mink ranch, was a little brown riding horse.

It seemed that Alvin was always bringing stray animals home. One day he came leading a billy goat up the driveway. But the goat couldn't stay very long. Only long enough to break out of the pasture and eat the clothes that Mama had hanging on the clothesline.

Much to Papa's dismay, Alvin also brought a crate of pigeons home that quickly made their messy home in the rafters of the barn. But one animal that he brought home that we all liked was Mickey, a mongrel dog. We didn't get to keep him for long, either, as he took to chasing our neighbor's cat-

4

tle. One day he came limping home, mortally wounded by a gunshot blast. He crawled under a bed and died soon after.

More cats and kittens than we could find names for roamed around the farm yard. Sometimes, instead of playing with my dolls, I would dress a kitten in the doll clothes and have a real live baby. I found out, too, that if I covered her eyes, she would fall fast asleep. But as soon as I laid her down, she would wake up and scamper away as fast as her little legs would take her.

With so many trees growing on our land, we were never in need of fuel to warm our house in winter. I can still hear Papa's saw as it ripped into the wood and the rhythmic chop of his ax as he split the logs into firewood. I can see him, too, coming in the kitchen door, his arms weighted down with the wood and clattering it into the woodbox. And, oh, how comforting it was to sit in front of that stove, my feet ice cold from playing out in the snow, resting on the open oven door.

After the snow melted in the spring, the woods and meadow were strewn with wildflowers of every color of the rainbow. The purple violets, orange and yellow cowslips, and the white lily of the valley made beautiful bouquets that I brought home to Mama. All through summer there were flowers to pick such as wild daisies, Jack-in-the-pulpit, black-eyed Susans and the dandelions that I braided into necklaces and chains that encircled my head like a crown.

But the flower I liked most of all but couldn't pick was the Lady Slipper, Minnesota's state flower. Early on, I got my first lesson in conservation when my brother, Milan, warned me, "Do not pick the Lady Slipper!"

His admonishment was so strong that I imagined someone was hiding behind a tree ready to pounce on me if I so much as touched one. So I had to be content just to sit and look at them. And as I looked, I imagined the fairies coming out of the woods at night wearing the tiny slippers on their feet and dancing merrily away in the moonlit meadow.

Now, whenever my husband and I take a drive out of the Twin Cities and I see a little farm away off in the distance, it magically becomes the farm in the valley. As we speed by on the freeway, the cows that I see grazing in their pasture, the swing swaying in the breeze, the dog running down the driveway and the wildflowers growing lavishly along the roadside, all help keep the spirit of the child that I was back then alive in me today.

GETTING TO KNOW YOU

Mama liked having babies and she saw to it that they were baptized soon after birth. When I was only three weeks old, she got me all dressed up, put a bonnet on my head, a hat on hers and carried me up and down the hills to our little country church, Zion Lutheran. It was a long walk and I would have been quite heavy by then so she must have been hot and tired when we arrived. And I certainly hope that a sympathetic neighbor gave us a ride back home.

I was given the name Dora Antona but a short while later Mama changed my middle name to Altona. I would have liked it to have remained Antona, which was after Anton, Papa's name, and I never quite forgave Mama for changing it until almost 59 years later. Then, during a chance conversation with the owner of the U-Neek Cottage, a gift shop in Vergas, Minn., I found out just how unique and significant the name Dora Altona is. Dora is the name of the township where I was born and when Vergas was first incorporated, it was named Altona.

I spent the next two months after my baptism sleeping, eating and watching my family. I found out I had worried needlessly about my brothers liking me. They all wanted to hold me and very often had to take care of me when Mama was busy. I was much too heavy for my sister, Eleanor, to carry me around so she would sit and rock me in the rocking chair while my brother, Loyal, stood nearby peering up at me from under the cap that was always on his head. I certainly didn't lack for attention. There was always someone to change my diaper and when I got hungry, all I had to do was cry and Mama was there to feed me.

Papa, Eleanor, Mama holding Loyal, Herbert, Alvin, LeRoy, and Milan—1936

Mama and Papa, who were thirty-eight and forty-six years old when I was born, must have been considered to be old by the standards of the thirties. But I never thought of them that way. To me, they were ageless and they didn't change much all through my school years and beyond.

Papa was deaf when I was born, the result of a bomb exploding too near him when he was in World War I. I feel as though I was born knowing that he couldn't hear me and it never hindered our relationship. I thought he could fix anything and I never hesitated to bring my broken dolls to him.

I was always able to make him understand what I needed and he always had an extra rubber band or whatever was needed to put my doll back together again.

Mama was "hard-of-hearing." I remember always having to speak loudly to her, a lifestyle that I naturally grew into. I never remember being embarrassed by her inability to hear well, probably because it wasn't an embarrassment to her, and I often served as her "interpreter." I'm sure that was the reason, as I grew older, that she liked having me with her when she shopped. When I think about the times when I didn't want to go with her, it makes me sad. I could have helped make life so much easier for her.

But other than being hearing impaired and sharing a love for music, Mama and Papa had little in common. Papa was tall, slim and dark complected with coal black hair. Mama was plump, fair complected with honey blonde hair and stood less

Mama, Papa, and me—1941

than five feet tall. Papa possessed a quiet, gentle nature and he remained calm throughout the fiercest summer storm. Mama liked to talk and sing. She never spared the rod when we kids were naughty and she became agitated at the first sign of an approaching storm.

Quite possibly, it was Mama's fear of having a new baby out in the country in the winter, where the roads often remained blocked for days after a snowstorm, that prompted her to have us live in Vergas my first winter. Had we remained in the country, I may not have made it into town in time for Dr. Boysen to remove a tumor that was growing on my neck before it ruptured.

The tiny scar that remains is proof of how significant my name is. It also serves as a reminder of yet another fast ride, one that gave me the chance to grow up so I could play with my brothers and sister. More importantly, that ride meant that I could continue on my journey.

LET'S PLAY PRETEND

I'm sure that Mama didn't hear, "What can we do now?" very often. We didn't have many "store bought" toys to play with. We had something much, much better—our imaginations. Most of our time, both in summer and winter, was spent outdoors. We ran, we jumped, we rolled, we climbed. Sometimes we even sat still looking for ships, cars and animals among the clouds. We went from one activity to another. We were never bored.

Many of the games we played were running games. In summer we played kick-the-can, run-sheep-run, red rover, hide-and-seek and tree tag. In winter, after we tramped through the fresh snow making the circle for fox and geese, we would play for hours.

Eleanor, me and Loyal—1941

Since I was the youngest, I was always the first to be "It." I remember standing up against a tree, my face hidden in my folded arms, trying to count to 50. I also remember crying when all the kids came in shouting, "Free" when I had barely started looking for them. The fleet-footed geese were difficult to catch, too, but eventually one would stumble and I was able to pounce on him. But, in no time at all, I was again caught.

But was I ever able to be the king of the hill? Certainly not. I remained a commoner always, never being able to reach the top of the hill before I was pushed back down.

The many hills that surrounded our valley were perfect for sliding. With a big enough push, we could reach the frozen slough at the bottom of the hill and then we would twirl round and round. But it took some skillful maneuvering on the part of the boys to keep from going belly-up.

In summer, that slough became Minnesota's number 10,001 lake where the boys fished from their homemade raft. The frogs, minnows and weeds that they caught were magically transformed into walleye, perch and sunfish. With Mama's permission, we even tried "swimming." But that was cut short when the bloodsuckers found our toes.

But of all the many different games we played, I was the happiest when I was playing house with my sister, Eleanor. We spent many hours caring for our babies, cleaning, washing clothes and cooking in the playhouse that our brothers built for us.

The shelves of our playhouse cupboard were always well stocked with "food" that nature provided. The red blossoms of the clover plant were strawberries; the white ones, potatoes; the large leaves of the basswood trees were bread and the seeds of the maple trees were bunches of bananas. We had lots of

Me and Loyal—1941

Me and Eleanor

cakes, pies and cookies, too, made from the flour of the earth and baked in our solar ovens.

Money was plentiful in our imaginary world as it grew on every tree. A maple leaf was a 10 dollar bill, an oak leaf a five dollar bill and the leaf of a poplar tree, a one dollar bill. Rocks of different sizes were transformed into nickels, dimes, pennies, quarters and half dollars.

No, we didn't have much in material things but I didn't mind because I didn't know any different. I made do with what I had and I was blessed with the greatest gift of all—my imagination. I could be anything I wanted to be. A sheep, a fox, a goose. A cowgirl, Indian maid or a mother. I swam in Lake Erie and I climbed Mt. Everest.

Now, whenever I take care of my grandson, Jeffery, and he says, "Let's play pretend, Grandma," my imagination once again springs to life. As I journey with him to his make-believe world, I'm able to keep the wonders of youth alive forever. We have more fun than if we had all the toys in a toy store to play with.

WIND IN THE WILLOWS

When Papa was a young man, he and his only brother, Hans, worked in the logging camps. After a hard day's work of hauling the timber through the deep snow, they would sit in front of the pot-bellied stove and entertain the other lumberjacks with music from their fiddle and harmonica.

It wasn't long before the news of these talented musicians spread over the countryside and they began to be asked to play at barn dances. It was at one of those dances that Mama first saw Papa. When she heard that a cook was needed at the lumber camp where he worked, Mama packed her bag and went to work there. They became better acquainted and eventually were married.

13

After Papa was married, Hans lived alone. Although I know he had many chances to marry, he remained a bachelor. When Papa lost his hearing, he had to give up playing the fiddle but when Hans came to visit, which was often, he entertained us for hours.

Papa and Hans

I don't think there was a country-western tune that he couldn't play. On and on he played the songs we requested, "Down in the Valley," "Nicolena," "Red River Valley," "On Top of Old Smoky," and ending with my favorite, "The Wabash Cannonball." He would cup his hand over the ends of his harmonica in just the right way to produce the sounds of the train's engine and whistle. The sounds that came gushing out were so real that if I closed my eyes, I could "see" the train coming round the bend.

I remember both Mama and Papa singing and many of the songs they taught me. "Billy Boy," a ballad about a young man who was courting a lady who was too young to leave her mother, was the favorite of all that Mama taught me. In hopes of preserving her Mother Tongue, she taught me some Norwegian songs but I'm afraid I failed to keep her heritage alive as I don't remember a single one today.

I do remember marching back and forth, a make-believe gun flung over my shoulder, singing, "Over There, Over There," an army song that Papa taught me. I had no idea where "over there" was but that didn't prevent me from singing at the top of my lungs. When we tired of singing that, we marched on singing another army song, "You're in the Army now." I don't know if I knew the words back then but for many years after, whenever I heard it, I became frustrated that I couldn't understand the line, "You'll never get rich by digging a ditch."

Saturday evenings were spent listening to the Grand Ole Opry, compliments of our battery-operated radio. I can still hear, like it was last night, Minnie Pearl's "I'm just so proud to be here," ring out over the thunderous applause when she was introduced. The hour we spent laughing with her and singing along with Roy Acuff, Ferlin Husky, Little Jimmy Dickens, Linda Lou and Kitty Wells sped by much too fast.

Thanks to my brothers, who were blessed with good voices and memories, we were entertained throughout the week. The only song they couldn't sing, not because they didn't know the words but because it was *my* song, was "You Are My Sunshine." Many times, just to get me going, they would sing it and the more I cried and carried on, the louder and longer they sang until, finally, Mama had to come to restore the peace.

A few blocks from where I live with my husband today, is a street named Wyldwood. At the end of the street, tucked in among residential homes, is a little church. I had a hard time swallowing the lump in my throat the first time I saw that church as it brought back to me the words of "The Little Brown Church in the Vale." The words of other songs we sang sprang to my mind—"What a Friend We Have in Jesus," "Jesus Loves Me," "That Old Rugged Cross," and many others. I could hear "Rock of Ages" being sung at the funerals of Grandma and Grandpa Johnson and at the graveside service of my little baby brother.

Then the memory of another elaborate funeral came to my mind—a funeral that my sister and I once had for some badly broken dolls. As we stood by the little graves that Papa had dug down by the willow trees, we solemnly lowered our heads and sang, "Rock of Ages, cleft for me."

The music we heard wasn't only that which came from Hans' harmonica, the Grand Ole Opry or from our church. Nature provided us with many lovely melodies. The wind played a beautiful melody as it weaved in and out of the willow trees. The crickets and frogs chirped and croaked in perfect harmony. The birds sang and the bees buzzed. The cows, horses, and Billy the Goat sang an out-of-tune melody. The water from the spring melt-off ping-pinged a piano tune as it gushed down over the rocks. I was blessed to be surrounded by these beautiful sounds of music and to be able to carry them with me on my journey.

A KNOT AROUND MY NECK

Forty acres wasn't enough land to provide for a family of nine so when Papa was finally awarded a government pension to compensate for his deafness, it made life a little easier.

What an exciting day it was when the mailman left the check in the mailbox. The boys hurried to finish their chores while Mama scurried around getting Eleanor, Loyal and me all dressed up for our trip into town. Then off went her apron, a hat went on her head and we ran down the hill and scrambled into the car.

The boys filled the radiator with water, cranked it to get it started and off we drove down the driveway. They made sure there was extra water and a spare tire along in case the radiator boiled over or we had a flat tire and I remember, many times, pulling over to the side of the road to use both.

Our first stop on reaching town was Olson's Grocery Store. After "taking care" of the previous month's grocery bill, Mama got busy picking out the groceries that were needed. She seldom bought anything fancy or ready made, just flour, sugar, oatmeal, coffee, rice, cocoa, macaroni, Jell-O, peanut butter and big galvanized pails of syrup. If she bought cookies they were either coconut washboards, which I didn't like, or Aunt Sally, a molasses rectangular shaped cookie with thick white frosting. I usually got a box of Cracker Jack that contained a real plastic toy and Henry Olson always placed a free bag of candy on the top of one of our grocery bags.

Then it was up the street to Lodin's Five and Ten Cent Store where we really could buy something for that amount. I didn't tag after Mama when she found her Evening in Paris or looked at the oilcloth tablecloths. I hurried to the back of the store and feasted my eyes on all the dolls and paper doll books. If there was any extra money, Mama sometimes bought us an inexpensive toy. One I remember was a little doll I once got which was just like Eleanor's doll except for hair color. I remember taking her out of the bag long before we were home and holding her in my arms.

When we got home, the boys helped Papa carry the groceries into the house. The kitchen cupboards were full once again with the staples that, when stretched, would have to last until our next trip into town.

Except for Mama's delicious potato dumpling soup, I don't think that my diet was the envy of anyone. I usually woke up to a breakfast of pancakes and syrup or a big bowl of oatmeal. Dinner, which was the noon meal back then and the biggest of the day, usually consisted of potatoes and macaroni, romegrot (milk mush) which I didn't like at all, rice with milk, sugar, cinnamon and a dab of butter or Mama's soup.

Mama usually used the leftovers of dinner to prepare supper, the evening meal. Mid-morning and afternoon lunches were also sit-down meals around the kitchen table. If a neighbor dropped in, Mama set the table with bread and jam, canned peaches or pears, Jell-O, cake and cookies. Then she stood by to make sure their cups were full of her strong, hot coffee.

Maybe I can give some credit for my healthy body to my early diet and maybe even to Mama's nursing skill, however crude they may have been.

Not long ago, when I heard the joke, "How do you keep a head cold from spreading?", I immediately thought of Mama, who as a young girl wanted to be a nurse. Way back then, Mama knew the answer. "Tie a knot around your neck."

That's exactly what she did whenever I had a head cold or a sore throat. First, she rubbed me down, from my ears to my tummy, with a thick layer of Vicks. Then she took the flannel rag that she had heating up on the stove, and placed it on my chest. Another warm rag was securely pinned around my throat. The tightness of the rag and the strong fumes that emanated from the Vicks-soaked rag, threatened to choke me. But surely, if any germs escaped beyond my throat, they succumbed before they reached my chest.

I had many earaches when I was little so I know the pain that a child with an ear infection endures when he pulls on his ear. There was no fast ride into town for a shot of penicillin in those days so, once again, I was at the mercy of one of Mama's sure-fire remedies that almost did set me on fire.

She scooped glowing live coals out of the stove and placed them in a fruit jar. Then she sprinkled sugar over the coals. When they began to burn with a thick, sweet-smelling smoke, she held the jar up to my ear. The pain did subside, whatever the reason, but I still wonder if it was harmful to my hearing.

When I reached the half-century mark and my sister and brothers began to reach retirement, I thought, until Alvin's sudden death, that we would all have long lives. Papa was 92 and Mama 89 at the time of their deaths. Neither had undergone surgery nor spent time in a hospital until their last years. Both ate lots of starchy foods and drank innumerable cups of strong, black coffee but neither ate much red meat. Was it that these foods balanced out the other or was it their Norwegian genes that gave them their healthy bodies?

Or was it the opportunity that they had of living out in the country? Back where everything grew naturally, the air was fresh and the water, which was drawn up from deep in the ground, sparkled because it had not yet been touched by man.

WE REGRET TO INFORM YOU

My very own memory, not something that was told to me, is of that fateful day, December 7, 1941, the day the Japanese bombed Pearl Harbor. I was not yet four years old but I remember it as if it was yesterday.

I remember standing off by myself, watching my brothers as they leaned in close to the radio so as not to miss a single word. I didn't understand what was happening but I instinctively knew that what they were hearing was both sad and serious.

I often wonder yet what went through Papa's mind when he was told the news. He must have relived again and again the events of World War I that robbed him of his hearing. He must have been hoping that by the time LeRoy and Milan were old enough to be drafted, the war would be over.

But it didn't end. Instead, it escalated and the age of registration was lowered to include all eighteen-year-olds. Milan and LeRoy registered, received their "Greetings" letters and shipped out shortly after Milan had married. Milan went to France and LeRoy to Italy.

A few months later, Mama's fear that the boys would be killed or wounded became reality when the dreaded "We regret to inform you" Western Union telegram arrived. Both were in a hospital far from home, Milan with a wound in his back and LeRoy in the arm.

There was no reasoning with Mama after that. She no longer liked "living in the woods" as she now called the country and she became dead set on leaving. She found an apartment in a big stucco house in Pelican Rapids and when school was let out in the spring, we moved in.

If Mama felt like a princess when she moved into our country home, the apartment must have made her feel like a queen.

LeRoy and me—1942

We had both a downstairs and an upstairs with a big hall that was a perfect place for playing paperdolls.

It had every modern convenience. With the touch of a finger, the dark rooms came to life. If we wanted a glass of water, we turned on a faucet. When we took a bath, the hot water came out of the other faucet and we could take our baths behind a locked door. But, best of all, was that we no longer had to take our little "trips" outdoors, something that I really dreaded in the dark of night.

On August 30, 1944, I celebrated my sixth birthday while living there. I could have started first grade that fall had I not contracted whooping cough. Instead of walking through town up to the schoolhouse with my brothers and sister, I sat looking out the window watching the neighbor-kids walk by. I remember well the violent spells of coughing that wracked my body and the brief respite after the whoops rose up from my chest.

I never did get well enough to begin school before we moved back into the country in early October. I must have remained ill for quite some time as I only attended country school for seven short days before we once again moved into town.

After having a taste of "city" living, Mama was unable to adjust back to living in the country. She again began looking for a place in town, this time a home to purchase.

One was found after only a short hunt. On October 23, 1944, Alvin's birthday, he along with Papa and Mama, loaded our belongings into a four-wheel trailer. A quick stop was made at the schoolhouse to get Eleanor, Loyal, Herbert and me. After a tearful good-bye to our friends and teacher, we hopped in the car and down the highway we went to begin, what would prove to be, an exciting new life style.

IT'S SPRING - THE MEADOW'S REBORN

It's Spring — *The meadow awakens to the warmth of the golden sun. The snow that had once been its blanket has melted and now it is gone.*

It's Spring — *The clover leaf pushes its fragile head up through the ground. With their leaflets, the meadow, they'll dress; pink flowers adorning the gown.*

It's Spring — *Wild flowers are blooming. Perfume gently floats through the air. With beauty, the meadow, they're grooming their garlands festooning its hair.*

It's Spring — *The meadow is reborn with all things so freshly renewed. The faded brown dress that she had worn is replaced with a green, yellow, blue.*

It's Spring — The Meadow's reborn!

Papa—1948

PAPA

Growing up is harder now, than many years ago.
The modern child has many toys, and is always on the go.
Back when I was growing up, Papa would teach us things.
To make-believe, and make our toys from boxes, sticks and
*   strings.*
Papa was in the army when he was twenty-eight
A bomb exploding close to him, proved to be his fate.
He finally got a pension, and learned some carpentry
*   skills.*
That helped him raise his family and pay the grocery bills.
During the Depression days, cash was hard to find.
We grew up without luxuries, but we didn't seem to mind.
Papa was always handy with tools and bits of wood.
He could take a broken toy and mend it just as good.
Papa was just a plain man, with no pretense or show.
He never joined a country club, or made a lot of dough.
He could make so many things, with his old pocket knife;
Whistles, slingshots, and other things, on which one couldn't
*   put a price.*
Papa chewed tobacco, he didn't smoke a pipe.
He was always philosophical, and never had a gripe.
If the neighbors were in need, he'd lend a helping hand.
And he was known as "Papa" by all his little friends.
Farming was his livelihood, although it wasn't big.
He'd hire out to farmers, who had a threshing rig.
He had a little garden, of corn, potatoes, beets,

25

And he would be out there hoeing, in ninety degree heat.
But, if the weather turned real bad,
He'd be out in his shed.
He wouldn't be in there working,
He'd be reading the newspaper instead.
Yes, Papa was real good to us,
When we were lass and lad.
And then one day he passed away, and left us feeling sad.
But I can feel him watching still,
I know he'd think he oughta,
And I still feel the influence of my beloved Papa.

TREES

Have you ever given thought to how important are the trees and to the part they played in your family's history? There were so many trees on which a swing was hung and here we would spend so many hours just having a lot of fun.

I remember the great, big, old, oak tree where Papa hung a tire. We always would want him to push us up higher and higher. I cannot forget the big basswood trees that gave us our playhouse bread or the money that grew on the tall maple trees which helped keep our dollies well fed. They played a big part in the games that we played; they were always a good place to hide. Some of them grew very close, side by side, for our many games of tree tag. They furnished the wood for the toys Papa made—the slingshots and whistles, the stilts and stick horses—and they served as the posts for Mama's clothes-line so our clothes could be hung in the nice bright sunshine.

I remember the grove of beautiful trees which grew on our uncle's farm. And on these trees, not one, but two hammocks were hung. And also the orchard of crab apple trees that furnished the apples Aunt Martha would can. I remember how thick the trees grew by the river and the ropes the boys tied up so high. They'd swing up and out and giving a shout, right into the water they'd dive.

How many trees had to be cut down to keep our houses warm? Or to dry all the soaking mittens that out in the snow we'd worn?

So many things are taken for granted until they are given some thought. To the Lord up above, for these trees that he gave, I say from my heart, "Thanks alot."

PART TWO

STAR LIGHT-STAR BRIGHT

I wished for many things. I wished for a bicycle and a pair of figure skates. I wished that I had a pretty name like my friend, Karen. I wished that I was beautiful, that my hair wasn't red and that my freckles would disappear. I wished that the noise in my head would go away. And I wished that I could hear better.

To be without some of the things you want is an indispensible part of happiness.

Bertrand Russell

The sun was brightly shining down from a clear blue Indian summer sky when I rode with my family through town and up the driveway to the house that would forever be "home" to me. I will always believe that God, in his wisdom, placed us there for it was the perfect place for both Papa and Mama.

It was located on the outskirts of town so Papa was able to have another big garden and if he chose, he could again raise animals. There were neighbors near by for Mama to visit and downtown was near enough for her to reach by walking.

I think whoever wrote, "You can take the boy (girl) out of the country, but you can't take the country out of the boy (girl)," had Mama and Papa in mind. Neither lost their love for the country. Mama didn't lose her country charm and Papa didn't lose his bib overalls with the red bandanna handkerchief hanging from the back pocket.

The big two-story white house, with a gabled porch, sat atop a hill and was surrounded by old, wiry oak trees. What both intrigued and puzzled me about the house was the number of doors it had. Not only did it have the customary front and back doors, it had three front doors. But by the time I left home, all four doors were closed off and Papa had replaced one in an entirely different spot.

Although the house was crudely wired with bare lightbulbs hanging from the center of each room, we did have electricity. We no longer had to rely on our battery-operated radio and Mama soon got an electric wringer wash machine and an electric iron. But some things remained the same.

City water did not yet reach our part of town so we had to continue to pump our water and heat it on our wood-burning stove that once again heated the house. And just as we did in the country, we resumed taking our little "trips" outside.

Down below the hill was a barn and several outbuildings. We didn't bring any of our farm animals along with us so, except for the cats that were living in the barn and the chickens Mama raised each summer, the buildings stood empty.

There was lots of open space for playing and a haymow full of hay just waiting for us. As soon as the boys discovered it, we unpacked our imaginations and joined the circus. With the hay as our safety net, we flew on ropes tied to the rafters from one end of the haymow to the other, pretending that we were trapeze artists. We would have liked to have stayed there playing forever but when Monday came we had to go back to school.

That time, when my brothers and sister walked up the road, I was with them. Mama didn't go with us. I suppose her hearing loss prevented her from doing so and the responsibility for getting me enrolled fell on Eleanor. And what a traumatic day it turned out to be for both of us.

She didn't take me directly to my first grade room. Instead, she brought me up to her sixth grade room to show me off to her teacher and friends. On the way back down, she tripped and stumbled down some steps. She didn't think she was injured until she fainted while my teacher was questioning her. She was taken home and I was left behind to cry in bewilderment.

At recess time, with all the attention that a new kid in school always gets, I recovered and got acquainted with my classmates. I didn't have any trouble finding my way home for lunch that day, either, as there were many helpful and curious older kids who wanted to help me. When I arrived home I found Eleanor, a sprained wrist resting in a sling that was tied around her neck.

When I think about my first year of school, I can't help but think how frustrated Miss Chesley must have been to have to put up with me. With five older brothers and a sister who taught me at home, I thought I already knew everything and I was overeager to show her just how smart I was.

I didn't like it when I was placed with the slowest readers. My hand was always waving in the air because I wanted Miss Chesley to find out that I had already read those books. I wanted to read all the time. She did move me rapidly from one group to the next but whether it was that I had mastered each one or if it was to give the other kids a chance to read, I don't know.

Thanks to my brother, LeRoy, who taught me how to write my name, penmanship wasn't any better. Quite possibly, it gave my teacher even more of a headache.

When she gave me a piece of paper and told me to write my name on all the lines, I did just that. I finished quickly and then sat back and waited for her to come and see what a good job I had done. I was pretty proud of myself and I just knew she would be proud of me, too. But I was terribly mistaken.

When she looked over my shoulder and saw that I had written my name in cursive, she took my paper away, gave me a clean sheet, printed my name at the top and told me to do it all over again.

I had a very difficult time learning to print the letter "r". I thought it should look the way my big, smart brother had taught me and I didn't like it when she told me that he was wrong. I didn't like my teacher much after that and I no longer tried to please her.

I don't remember my brothers or sister ever talking about having their hearing tested in country school so possibly it was a new experience for us all when the county nurse visited. More than half a century has passed and I can remember my first hearing test as well as I remember my last one in 1996.

The nurse set up shop in the hallway outside the first grade room. One by one, we were called out of the room, placed on a high chair and a set of heavy ear phones was clamped over our ears.

I remember getting alot of attention, probably due to Papa's and Mama's hearing disabilities. Even at such a young age, my instincts told me that I wouldn't be able to hear the sounds. When I did hear the loudest and then each consecutive sound, I was excited and proud. I still recall, too, how happy Miss Chesley and the nurse were as they told me that all was well and then sent me on my way.

I didn't attend Sunday morning church services until I was old enough to go alone. That was one other place where Mama and Papa didn't go because of their hearing problems but just as Mama wanted all her kids baptized, she wanted us to go to Sunday school. As soon as we got settled in public school and found a church in town, she sent us off to Sunday school. That is another "first" that I remember well.

I arrived early and helped my teachers set up the little chairs in a circle. I thought it was so much fun to sing the songs and listen to the Bible stories. I know my faith took root that day.

That first year of living in town was exciting and so different from living in the country. When school was let out for the summer, I got my report card promoting me on to the second grade. At times I still wonder if, like reading, Miss Chesley promoted me on my ability or if she couldn't bear to cope with me through another year.

IN VICTORY THERE WAS SORROW

My sister, brother and I didn't waste any time in exploring the neighborhood. Our flat bottomland wasn't a good place to play cowboys and Indians so when we discovered that there weren't any animals in our neighbor's pasture, we moved in. The ravines, hills and trees made it the perfect place for setting up camp and because it adjoined our property, it was within ear and eyesight of Mama.

The war was still going on and, even though Milan and LeRoy were no longer in combat, Mama was nervous. She didn't want us wandering far from home in case our little town was attacked. It seems very unlikely to me today that it would have happened but back then it was a real concern and fear.

It was a very uncommon sight to see just one airplane fly over town so when Mama saw three come flying together from the west, she was struck with terror. I saw her excited many times after that but never as excited as she was that day when she came running down the hill, pointing up at the sky.

When we looked up and saw the airplanes we knew what to do, either from drills at school or watching news reels at the movies. We ran to the barn and pasted our bodies up against the wall.

No bombs fell. The planes flew on. I know that I was frightened. I don't know about Eleanor but Loyal still maintains that he wasn't. He was only pretending, caught up in the excitement of a big adventure.

If Loyal wasn't afraid that day, I'm quite sure that he, like the rest of my family, was afraid the night of an air raid drill. As we sat in total darkness, the curtains pulled tight, we could hear the sirens and see the search lights flit across the sky. For some unknown reason, Mama was calm that night. She assured us that there wasn't any danger and that "they" were looking for a bank robber.

I have other memories of the war years. I pushed and Loyal pulled a wagon as we scavenged for scrap iron. And I remember well the day that LeRoy's Purple Heart, which he was awarded for being wounded, arrived in the mail. I didn't know the significance of it. I only knew that it was the prettiest thing I had ever seen.

Every chance I had, I took it out of its satin-lined box and held it in my hands. I did it so many times that, although I never had the courage to ask, I wonder if there was anything left of it by the time LeRoy got home.

But of all the memories of the war years, V-J Day, August 15, 1945 is the most memorable of all. Not for the happiness it brought but for the sorrow my family endured that day.

If I didn't yet know where babies came from, I found out one day earlier in the summer during a visit from Aunt Annie. Annie, who was Papa's sister, had been born deaf and as a young girl attended Faribault School for the Deaf where she learned sign language. So when she playfully patted Mama on her stomach and then rocked an imaginary baby, I knew what she said. Mama was going to have a baby!

The two months of waiting for the baby was a happy and exciting time. When the neighbors heard the news, they brought over beautiful little baby clothes. There were sweaters and caps, booties, soakers, kimonos and blankets. Our baby was going to be the best dressed baby in town.

We thought of names for the baby, too, and Mama decided on Linda Lou for a girl and Dennis for a boy. But we weren't to have either one. In the early morning of V-J Day, Mama gave birth to a stillborn son, a tiny casualty of the stress that the war brought Mama.

Quite likely, we were the only unhappy family in Pelican Rapids that day. Instead of going downtown to celebrate with the revelers, Papa, Eleanor and I walked straight through on the way to our pastor's home to make arrangements for the funeral.

A few days later, I stood with my family by his little grave, bowed my head and sang, "Rock of Ages, cleft for me."

Precious Memories

We all were deeply disappointed not to have that little baby boy but we did have the consolation of knowing that Milan and LeRoy would soon be coming home safely to us. My brother, Alvin, left for the service the day that LeRoy came home.

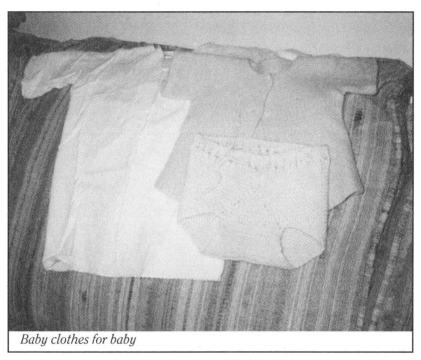

Baby clothes for baby

Milan was the first to arrive and he joined his wife, Leona, and son, Gary, whom he had not yet seen. Then, early one morning soon after Milan arrived, LeRoy came. We were all in the kitchen getting ready for school when Eleanor saw him walk by the window and exclaimed, "LeRoy is home!"

School was forgotten for the day as we stayed home and got reacquainted. I was only four years old when LeRoy left and I was a big girl of seven and in the second grade when he returned. He brought lots of things home to show us. C-

Rations (army food), trinkets, mementos of the war and gifts. Mine was a tiny gold locket on a chain.

But I wasn't to have that, either. I wore it to school the next day and as I proudly showed it to my teacher, a classmate pulled on the chain and it broke. Another day that had started so happily ended with me in tears. If it hadn't been for Miss Nicholson, my wonderful teacher that year, things would have been much worse. Her kindness brought me through that day and many more and the memories I have of her are very precious still.

Second grade: Miss Nicholson, teacher; I am in the second row—way to the left—1945

Every morning when I arrived at school, she would be standing by her classroom door, a smile on her face, welcoming her students. She possessed all the ingredients that go into making a good teacher. She was patient, understanding, cheerful, kind and she made learning a fun experience. She treated all her students fairly and she expected the same from them. She did not tolerate anyone making fun of another, a trait that certainly helped me one winter day.

I don't know why I had to wear boys' buckle overshoes that year. The only reason I can think of was because of the rubber shortage. But it didn't matter to me because I seldom got anything new so even getting new boys' overshoes was a treat. That is until, by accident, I wore someone else's overshoes home one day. Those, of course, belonged to a boy.

The next morning, I was the center of attention as my classmates gathered around me in the cloak room while Miss Nicholson straightened them out. I was embarrassed but thanks to the understanding way it was handled, not one classmate teased me.

But no matter, I no longer liked those overshoes after that. I begged and begged Mama to buy me a pair of girls' boots. Just in time for the spring thaw, I got a pair of shiny red girls' boots that I didn't waste any time on breaking in.

On the way home from school, I found the deepest puddle and waded in. Up and over the tops the water rushed in. Luckily, Mama wasn't home when I slushed into the house. My brother, Herbert, pulled them off, shoes and all, and set them behind the stove to dry out. By morning, with Mama no more the wiser, they were dry and ready for another day.

Oh, yes, I liked school and Loyal, who was in the fourth grade, must have, too. We didn't like being absent even when we were sick. Not even the chicken pox was going to keep us home for long.

As soon as we began to feel better, we started to beg Mama—I was getting good at that—to let us go back. She either grew weary of having us underfoot or got tired of our begging, for she covered our pox with powder—or was it another of her nursing remedies—and said, "Go!"

We weren't gone long. With one look at me, Miss Nicholson took my hand and led me out the door. As we rounded the corner, we met Loyal coming with his teacher. Our teachers had a quick conference and sent us packing for home.

We weren't about to spend the beautiful spring day sitting in the house. We went straight out into Halbakken's pasture and built the biggest and best camp that we had ever made. And it was woe to the neighbor kids who came out and joined us when school was over that day.

IT'S ALL IN MY HEAD

My third through sixth grades are a hodgepodge of memories that whirl and twirl through my mind in disarray. I remember the names of my teachers but very little about them or many events of those days.

I continued to like school and learning came easy to me until I tried to learn the multiplication tables. No matter how hard I tried, I just could not memorize them.

About that same time, I was hit on my head by a swing during recess and needed stitches to close the wound. So maybe I can put the blame on the bump on my head for what I did. Until then, I had been a pretty well-behaved little girl.

When my teacher gave us an oral quiz, I was well prepared. I copied the multiplication tables onto a piece of paper and placed it in my desk directly under the ink well hole in the corner. I was rolling right along until Elaine, the girl who sat in front of me, discovered what I was doing and tattled on me.

My paper was confiscated. I failed the test and I was chastised in front of all my classmates. That was the end of my cheating days. I worked hard. I took the flashcards home and one day it all "clicked." From then on, mathematics was my "thing." Maybe, too, that bump contributed to a bit of naughtiness during music class one day. We learned a new song, "The Donkey and the Cuckoo." Half of the class was donkeys while the other half was cuckoos and during the chorus sang either "cuckoo" or "hee haw."

Well, my friend, Kay, and I were so enthralled with the song that we continued right on hee hawing and cuckooing long after our music class was over. Our teacher warned us but we didn't listen. She finally had to separate us. Kay was put in the back row and I in the front. Even then, we kept it up for a while. Whenever I looked back at her, she would say, "Cuckoo." Something good did come out of it though. That was the end of singing "The Donkey and the Cuckoo."

Itasca National Park: Cousin Clarence, LeRoy, Cousin Molly and me, Eleanor, Herbert and Loyal—1947

What with all the head injuries, the bump from the swing and being hit in the mouth with a baseball bat, and the illnesses I endured, earaches, the tumor and tonsillitis, I guess I can justifiably say, "It's all in my head."

I grew out of the earaches and right into tonsillitis with fevers so high I became delirious. I remember once being so hot that I went running to Mama screaming that my bed was on fire. A telephone call, from our neighbor's phone, brought

Dr. Korda to the house with his doctor's bag that contained a dose of penicillin.

But the injury that I recall most of all is the gash that I received on my forehead, the result of my cousin Clarence's folly and my stubbornness while staying on my Uncle Gilbert's farm.

A PENNY FOR YOUR THOUGHTS

There were three places on Uncle Gilbert's farm that I didn't like—the hen house, the barn and the dark, dank cellar.

I didn't like the noisy clucking of the chickens so whenever I went with Aunt Annie to gather eggs, I stayed outside the door. When I went along with Aunt Martha to the barn at milking time, I went straight to the separating room and stayed there until the last cow was safely back in the pasture. And I would not go down into the cellar by myself.

One day I said, "No," when Martha asked me to go down to get a jar of sauce while Eleanor and I were staying out there. But when Eleanor said she would go, I was right behind her.

She was ahead of me on the way back up the cellar steps and when she stepped up into the kitchen, Clarence told her to shut the cellar door. She did so just as my head came up into view and a long protruding nail on the cellar door ripped a gash across my forehead.

The scar that it left on my forehead, which has always been covered by my hair, tells me that a doctor's attention would have been welcomed that day but no trip was made into town. Instead, Uncle Gilbert went alone and came back with a supply of salve and bandages and a big bag of candy that I wasn't too willing to share with Clarence and Eleanor.

That is the only really unpleasant memory I have of the farm. I feel so blessed to have had such a nice place to spend so many weeks of my summer vacations.

I can honestly say, too, that Aunt Martha and Uncle Gilbert were the biggest influence in my life. They always expected the best of me and I tried very hard to please them. They had been married for many years by the time I was born so they were more like a Grandma and Grandpa to me. They lived with their son, Clarence, and Aunt Annie on the farm that was a few miles west of Pelican Rapids. And what a beautiful farm it was.

Tall pine trees encircled the house, guarding it. Behind the pines, sweetpeas of every color of the rainbow wove in and out of the mesh wire fence. Hollyhocks, with blooms bursting down their stems, strove to stand upright. And Martha's snowball bush, that was emblazoned with huge clusters of tiny white blossoms, complemented the flower beds that were scattered around the yard.

Two weather worn hammocks, hanging in the grove of old twisted oak trees, swayed in the breeze. Crab apple trees, their branches weighted down with ripening fruit, provided the backdrop for the little white house that sat nestled in the wonderland.

From the early morning's "Cock-a-doodle-do" of the roosters to the "Now I lay me down to sleep," when Martha tucked me into bed, my day was busy. There was always something to do. I helped bake cookies and doughnuts, I helped with the canning, I washed dishes and I put photographs in the album. And I learned how to sew on a treadle sewing machine.

Martha gave me a piece of feed sack material and helped me cut out a dress for my doll. Then she sat alongside me and showed me how to pedal the treadle and guide the fabric under the needle. I still have that dress and the doll it was made for. It certainly would not have won a ribbon at the county fair but Aunt Martha was proud of me and I still think it's the prettiest dress my doll ever had.

I spent many hours of quality time with my aunt Annie, too. When I think about her now, I realize just how much like her I am. Like me, she also was curious and wanted to know what was going on around her.

Even if Martha had tried, she could not have prevented Annie from participating in our conversations. Like me, she was persistent, always asking Martha what others said. Ultimately, Aunt Martha's hands and voice worked in unison as she kept Annie informed.

Me and Rachel—1949

Annie loved having us kids come to visit. Then she, too, could be a child along with us, if just for a little while. I can see her as if it were yesterday. Her face was alive with emotion and small utterances and peals of laughter would emerge from her lips in her excitement as she entertained us with homespun magic.

With a few folds of a simple hanky, she could make a tiny mouse or twin babies sleeping in a blanket. A string threaded through the holes of a coat button magically became an airplane that we whirled and twirled around the kitchen. But the most fun of all was playing cat's cradle, passing the string back and forth from her hands to mine.

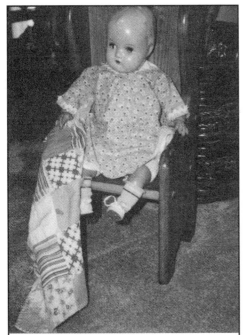

Rachel wearing the first doll dress that I made. With doll quilt made by Aunt Annie

Bedtime came early on the farm but I didn't mind because I loved the bedroom that Eleanor and I shared. The big bed with the thick feather pillows was as close to luxury as I'll ever be. And to awaken and find a pitcher of hot water waiting for me on the antique dry sink certainly made me feel like a queen.

But when Eleanor outgrew her visits to the farm, the nights alone in that room were far from pleasant. They were probably some of the longest nights of my life as I lay listening, every hour, to the chime of the clock float up the stairs.

Even more disturbing was listening to Buster, the farm dog, bark when a commotion in the farmyard woke him up. I would work myself into a dither and lay trembling as I expected someone to walk through the doorway and carry me away.

One night I cried so hard that Aunt Martha heard me and came upstairs and brought me down to sleep with her and Uncle Gilbert. The following night and anytime I spent out there after that, my bed was the living room couch. There, only a few feet from Aunt Martha, I was able to sleep, oblivious to what was going on outside in the farmyard.

Cousin Clarence, Aunt Martha, Uncle Gilbert; small photo—Annie.

Facing page: Uncle Gilbert's farm

Many memories will be with me always. I remember the smell of Uncle Gilbert's cigar, the pink peppermints that Annie always had in her room, the hustle and bustle to get ready to go to the county fair, the shaking and rattling of the thresh machine as it rolled up the driveway. And the "A penny for your thoughts" that Cousin Clarence so often asked me.

So many times I would sit quietly, deep in thought or maybe because I couldn't hear clearly when everyone else was talking, until Clarence broke into my reverie by asking, " A penny for your thoughts, Dora."

I could only smile, unable to tell him anything. Today, if he could ask me, he'd have to sit a while and he'd have to have all the pennies from heaven to pay me and then he may not yet have enough.

PLEASE, GOD, NOT ME TOO

Many changes took place in my family the year before I started junior high. I began to notice that, with each visit, Milan was losing his hearing. LeRoy moved to Hibbing, Minn. to work in the iron mines. There he met and married Louella. Alvin married Olive and Herbert joined the Air Force and was stationed in California. He, too, got married and his wife's name was Phyllis.

Loyal began his freshman year and Eleanor, who was in her junior year, dropped out.

Once again, the loud environment at home gets the credit for covering up her hearing loss. When the news spread like wild fire through school that she quit because she couldn't hear well, I was as surprised as anyone.

Not once during the times we spent together playing with our dolls and paperdolls, drawing, playing games or writing poetry did I suspect that she couldn't hear me. And if the volume of the radio was turned up when we listened together, I didn't give it any thought.

Many hours were spent listening to one program after another. Week nights we listened to "The Adventures of Archie Andrews" and his friends, "Our Miss Brooks," "The Great Gildersleeve," and the quiz shows, "Name That Tune" and "Groucho Marx."

Sunday afternoons we sat glued to the radio listening to one mystery program after another. We heard the squeaking door of "Inner Sanctum." We heard the Shadow ask us, "Who knows what evil lurks in the hearts of man? The Shadow knows," and then his blood curdling laughter. And we heard the Lone Ranger ride off with his "Hi yo, Silver, away" after he had brought law and order to a town.

And, just as my grandsons, and my sons before them, watch Saturday morning cartoons, my sister and I listened to "The Teddy Bear Picnic" on the radio. We heard Froggie plunk his magic twanger and we heard Buster Brown tell us that he and his dog, Tide, lived in a shoe.

Perhaps that was one of the first signs that I, too, was losing my hearing. After thinking for 50 years that Buster Brown's dog's name was Tide, I now know that it was Tige. But before I became aware that I could no longer hear well, something else began to take place. That, too, was "in my head."

It was unnoticeable during my waking hours but in the quiet of the night, noise crept into my head. Quietly at first, it then built into a crescendo as loud as the roaring of a waterfall. It frightened me but I kept it to myself. I learned to control it somewhat by clenching my teeth and holding my breath over and over again until I fell asleep.

Then, as if synchronized with the physical changes that were taking place in my body, I realized that my hearing was also changing. That, too, I kept to myself.

49

Often times, before I went to bed, I would sit on the floor by the window in my room and watch for the first star of night so I could wish upon it.

> *Star Light - Star Bright*
> *First star I see tonight.*
> *I wish I may, I wish I might*
> *Have the wish, I wish tonight.*

I wished for many things. I wished for a bicycle and a pair of figure skates. I wished I had a pretty name like my friend, Karen. I wished I was beautiful, that my hair wasn't red and that my freckles would disappear. I wished that the noise in my head would go away and that I could hear better.

MODERNIZATION

The grass wasn't fertilized and it was thick with clover
And it took a day to mow it with the old push lawn mower.
But things were good out on that farm,
So why did modernization have to come?

Milk wasn't pasteurized; butter wasn't graded either
And to skim the cream from off the top, they used a separator.
But things were good out on that farm.
So why did modernization have to come?

Sauce wasn't bought in stores back then, instead it was home canned
And the work got done in fall without a cooling fan.
But things were good out on that farm.
So why did modernization have to come?

Fancy yard goods were not purchased, printed feed sacks made a dress
And it took alot of energy, that old foot feed to press.
But things were good out on that farm.
So why did modernization have to come?

Lefsa was made atop an old wood stove, not on an electric pan
And the fires were kept burning with wood they carried in by hand.
But things were good out on that farm.
So why did modernization have to come?

*They hadn't begun to combine; farmers shared a thresh
    machine
And the men worked very hard, until the fields stood clean.
But things were good out on that farm.
So why did modernization have to come?*

*Yes, times were hard away back then, but no one knew "no
    better"
And they worked and played and went without and it didn't
    really matter
'Cause things were good out on that farm.
So why did modernization have to come?*

PART **T**HREE

TRUE **G**RIT

Before I began to write about my high school days, I sat back and became reacquainted with the girl I was back then. As the memories came to my mind, something happened that never once did I allow to happen to myself then. Tears filled my eyes and ran unchecked down my cheeks. I didn't think so then but I do now. I was given a hard row to hoe.

If you can give something a name and a shape, you can have power over it. If it remains nameless and shapeless, it will have power over you.

Native American Proverb

Before I began to write about my high school days, I sat back and became reacquainted with the girl I was back then. As the memories came to my mind, something happened that never once did I allow to happen to myself then. Tears filled my eyes and ran unchecked down my cheeks. I didn't think so then but I do now. I was given a hard row to hoe.

Fortunately, I received several useful tools from Mama and Papa. From Papa came his patience, self-control and tolerance. Mama gave me high self-esteem, perseverance and a sense of humor. Along with those, I added two of my own, creativity and acceptance.

I certainly didn't deny to myself that I was hard-of-hearing. I met it head-on but it was my secret. I did not want to share it with anyone. Since Mama and Papa and now Milan and Eleanor were all affected, I figured it was something that ran in the family. I accepted it as a way of life.

There were many reasons why I didn't want to confide in anyone. I didn't want Mama and Papa to feel responsible and I didn't want to be a burden to them. Hard as it is for me to admit even today, I also feared that Mama would be angry with me if she knew.

I certainly didn't want to be pitied. More than anything else, I just wanted to be normal. I didn't want anyone to think I was dumb, dull or dimwitted, the stigmas that went along with being deaf at that time.

Like Eleanor, my loss, too, went undetected at home. When I was with my friends, I did my best to bluff myself through. Long before kids were warned not to speak to strangers, I tried to avoid them. Sometimes that wasn't possible and I was caught red-handed.

By the tone of a voice, I was able to differentiate between a question and a statement so I often "played it by ear." I didn't feel any pressure to respond to a statement other than to smile and pretend interest but questions weren't so easy. After the initial, "What?", if I still hadn't heard, I would resort to the proverbial "yes," "no," or more often, "I don't know" and then blush and walk away, leaving them to wonder, "What's wrong with her?"

The misunderstandings, when what I heard was something other than what was said, were even more traumatic as they often times made me even more embarrassed. I remember well one of the first times that happened to me.

My friend, Doreen, was late meeting me to go to the school circus. When she finally arrived and told me she was late because she had been at choir practice, I was puzzled because I knew she wasn't in the choir. I didn't say anything but later, when she mentioned her back, I realized she hadn't been at choir practice. She had been to the chiropractor. I went unscathed that time but not so when I told my teacher about a new game I had heard about.

When my brother, Loyal, described the new game Crazy Eights—not to be confused with the card game—he had played the previous night, I couldn't wait to get to school to tell my teacher all about it.

When I said it was a parlor game and then described it as a guessing game with song titles, names of movies, etc., acted out in pantomime, she looked at me, a puzzled look on her face, and said "I think you mean charades."

Indeed, I was describing charades and it became a favorite game of mine. Other than the brief time when I had to be the mime, I was completely at ease. I could ask as many questions as I wanted and I didn't have to strain to hear the answers. I "heard" them with my eyes.

But my eyes weren't any help when I played "gossip" at a boy-girl birthday party. Then my secret came close to being uncovered.

I'm sure you are familiar with the game. One guy whispers a message to the girl sitting next to him, she whispers it to the guy next to her and on and on until it reaches the last person in the circle who then reveals it to everyone.

Well, the message didn't get beyond me. I couldn't hear it so I creatively made up my own. I got away with it the first time by pretending silliness but not the second time. The birthday boy became suspicious and told his dad. Not much was said. The kids weren't concerned. They were at the party to have fun, not to talk about my hearing.

But as I got older, I often became the life of the party not because it came naturally to me but out of necessity.

So many times while I was deaf and since my hearing was restored, I have been asked the question, "Why is the quality of your voice so good after being deaf for so long?"

My answer to that, and I say it with total sincerity, is that I never stopped talking. I learned early on that if I did most of the talking, I would be in control of the conversation and would know the subject. Thus, there would be less for me not to hear. I also tried to remember as many jokes as I could. Then I didn't have to pretend to laugh at the jokes of others when I couldn't hear them.

Although I would have liked to have been involved in speech or drama or to have sung in the chorus or played an instrument in the band, I shied away from those activities. Instead, I participated in those that called for action rather than speech. I was a tomboy and I had some natural athletic ability that helped me there.

I got my wish for ice skates when my brother, LeRoy, bought me a pair when I was in the seventh grade and I almost wore them out that first year. When summer arrived, I hung out at the surrounding lakes and then in town when a part of the river was developed and made into a swimming pool.

I joined GAA (Girls Athletic Association) where I was in my realm both as a team member and as an official. I even tried a bit of cheerleading but I gave that up after only a few "Rah! Rah! Rahs!" I was not cut out to be a leader.

Rain on the Roof

I didn't need my teachers to tell me to pay attention. I knew I had to. For me to make it through each day, I always had to be alert. I couldn't whisper and cut up like my classmates for, if I did, I was lost. I always had to stay one step ahead of my teachers and try to anticipate just what their next action might be.

During a classroom discussion, I didn't wait to be called on. If I heard the question and knew the answer, my hand shot up in the air. When we were taking turns reading out loud, I paired the students off with the paragraphs so I would know what I would be reading. Then I would mark the paragraph, read at my own pace, and watch to see when the person in front of me was finished reading.

Even insignificant things like answering roll call or giving my grade to the teachers after a quiz was a major problem for me. But I got around that by knowing who would be called ahead of me and then watching until they had been called on.

Any reference that was made to hearing or the ear sent bad vibes through me. Except for remembering the names of the three tiny bones located in the middle ear—the hammer, anvil and stirrup—the study of the ear in health class is a total blank to me. I was so vulnerable that even having to write an essay titled "Rain on the Roof" upset me. Since I didn't remember what rain on the roof sounded like, it took a lot of thinking to find something I was comfortable with. I still have that essay, yellowed with age, that I want to share with you.

The first thing that caught my eye when I took it out of my memento box was that it was make-up work. I wondered if I really was sick or was I stalling for time? I did get a good grade: B/B for both contents and structure but the remark at the end of the report intrigued me the most.

"Good and original. I like it. However, some of your sentences are cumbersome."

I still have that problem with writing today.

A SECRET NO MORE

My vulnerability became so great that when I heard the news of the imminent arrival of the nurse to test my hearing, I couldn't face it. No matter how creative I was, I couldn't, short of pretending that I could hear, scheme my way out. So I pretended something else or maybe I actually was sick by then. Anyway, I stayed home.

But it was only a temporary solution, one that only succeeded in bringing me more attention.

When I passed the gymnasium a few weeks later and saw the audiometer set up, I knew I was caught. Sitting in my classroom, waiting for the knock on the door that would call me out, was like waiting for a summons to appear in court.

I went through the testing and was given a letter to bring home. But it didn't get there. I threw it away instead, something else that I didn't get away with.

A few weeks later, as I was passing Principal Strinden's office, he called me in and questioned me. I think I was honest and told him I didn't bring the letter home but he didn't trust me with another. He mailed it.

I really believe that the letter was how Mama and Papa learned that one more of their children was hard of hearing. Mama wasn't mad at me. She promptly took me to see Dr. Korda who recommended that I have a tonsillectomy.

On the day before Thanksgiving Day, 1952, I underwent surgery. I expected to wake up, my hearing magically restored, and I think because of my past history of tonsillitis that Dr. Korda also was hopeful. But, of course, my hearing didn't improve. I no longer got the sore throats but it progressively became worse.

Sharon Smith, my audiologist, once asked me, "Did they want you to get a hearing aid?"

No one ever approached me on the subject, but had anyone offered to buy me one, I would have refused to wear it.

My reasons for not wanting to are the same as those I had for not telling anyone that I was losing my hearing. Mama and Papa and, probably by then, my closest friends, were the only ones who knew. I was not yet ready to confide in others and I became so adamant on keeping it a secret, that I went out of my way to avoid any confrontation.

I remember so well the day a salesman came to the house to see Mama. As soon as I found out he was there to fit Mama with a hearing aid, I went outside. I went as far away from the house as I could get and began to mow the lawn.

A short while later, I looked up at the house and saw him motioning me to come. I had no choice but to do as he wanted and I followed him into the house.

He told me to say something to Mama. I did and, lo and behold, she heard me. She purchased the aid and there was a tremendous change in her. But it was also a confusing time as she kept it in a covered dish in the cupboard as much as she wore it.

But probably the biggest reason for not wanting to wear a hearing aid was that I became interested in the opposite sex and surely no boy would want to date a girl who wore a hearing aid.

I WANT TO GO WITH YOU

I spent countless hours standing in front of the old mirror that hung above the kitchen sink, trying to make myself beautiful. My hair was still red but I kept it looking nice, my clothes were nice enough and my freckles had disappeared but still not one boy wanted me to be his girl friend.

Oh, they were my friends. We had fun together in groups at school and church, we sat together at athletic events, and I helped them with their schoolwork but it was always someone else they took to a movie or danced with at the school dances.

When Lila and David, Stephen and Patty, Ardis and Glenn, Joann and Dave began to pair up and go steady, I really felt left out. But now when I think about it, it's quite possible that some of my social problems were my own fault. Maybe the boys thought I wasn't interested in them just as I thought that they weren't interested in me.

Whenever I was caught alone with a boy and he began to talk to me, I recoiled in fear, thinking that I wouldn't hear him. If they thought I was shy, standoffish or even weird, they had every right to think so.

Once again, I had to compensate. Just as I had done with the Lady slippers that I couldn't pick, I sat back and stared at the boys. One boy, named Kenny, on whom I had a giant crush, got it the most. I stared and stared. So much, in fact, that had I been bionic then, like I am now, his shirt might have burst into flames and burned a hole through his back.

My best friends, Avis and Betty, weren't having any luck with the boys either. When Betty got a job at the local theatre and Avis started working as a waitress at the Uptown Hotel and Cafe, they had many opportunities to meet boys from neighboring towns. There was often an extra boy along for me and that was how I got my first steady, a boy named Don.

He must have wanted a steady just as much as I did for the entire procedure of exchanging class rings was accomplished in the first hour of our first date. I didn't hear any bells ring or see any flashing lights so it surely wasn't love at first sight.

Oh, he was nice and certainly good looking enough but I instinctively knew that I wasn't doing the right thing. But it did my ego good to know that a boy actually found me attractive enough to want me to wear his class ring. It was okay, too, to have a ring that I could wrap tape around, just like the other girls in school.

We got along okay and we did have fun together. Conversing with him was easy, too, as much of the time spent together was in the confines of his car, driving to basketball games and back and forth between his hometown and mine.

Gradually, disenchantment set in. My extra-curricular activities began to interfere with our dates and I didn't want to give them up. But I didn't initiate our breakup. He did.

I did feel sad and even a bit mortified. I shed a few tears and moped around home and school for a few days but I felt relieved too. I was again free to do as I wanted and when he began to date my best friend's sister, it didn't bother me at all. Then, too, I was better able to concentrate on my school work. My hearing was getting worse and I knew that if I was going to graduate, I would have to gather all my wits about me.

ENDURING CHALLENGE

When I was a little girl, I knew that I wanted to be a teacher and when I got older I knew what I wanted to teach. I wanted to be an English teacher. But when my hearing began to get bad, I faced reality. Even if there had been financial help for me, I would not be able to bluff my way through another four years of school.

I didn't give any thought to what I would do after I graduated. I just wanted to graduate. I didn't choose the classes with my future in mind. I chose those taught by the teacher I was familiar with and those that would be the least difficult for me. But no matter how carefully I chose, I once found myself in a very embarrassing situation.

I had always wanted to learn to type. From the time I was in grade school and would hear the clatter of the typewriters when I walked by the typing room, I was fascinated by them. So it was quite natural for me to take the class when I became old enough.

Everything was going great my first day. I heard my teacher, Mrs. Stadum, well and I was actually making words appear on my paper. The period was coming to an end and I was feeling really good about myself. Then disaster struck!

Mrs. Stadum asked, "Whose bell rang?"

I hadn't heard a bell ring. I wasn't even aware that a typewriter had a bell but I looked around the room along with the other students anyway.

I found out that a typewriter did, indeed, have a bell and, of course, it had been mine that she had heard. Oh, yes, I was embarrassed that time. I would have liked to have had the floor open up and swallow me.

But then I *did* hear a bell, this time a friendly one. I didn't wait around to find out where the typewriter's bell was located. I gathered up my books and hurried out the door. I went straight to the school office and asked to be released from typing class. The only other available class was geometry. I signed up for that.

The next day when I walked into my new class, I was welcomed by my favorite teacher, Mr. Haugen. There were umpteen boys in class and only two girls so I felt welcome, at least by the girls. I was back in chartered waters and it was a class that proved very useful in obtaining a job in the distant future.

Bookkeeping class was a breath of fresh air compared to most of my other classes. From my desk at the back of the room, I was able to hear my teacher, Mr. Fauteck, very well. Then too, from that vantage point, and not having to keep my mind on what was going on in the classroom, I had more time to stare at my friend, Kenny.

I didn't have to worry about my hearing as most of the period was spent keeping a set of books. But one day, near the end of the school year, I didn't have any books to keep. When I went to get them out of my locker, I couldn't find them. I was sure I hadn't taken them home the previous night or left them laying somewhere. I didn't have any idea where they were. I turned the locker upside down and even looked in the lockers of my classmates. They were nowhere to be found.

With only a few days remaining of the school year, there certainly wasn't time to complete another set and with my final grade based on the work that I had done, both Mr. Fauteck and I were in a quandary.

But one morning, just as mysteriously as they had disappeared, my books were back in my locker. I did find out who had taken them but I was so relieved to have them back that no confrontation was made. Besides, I felt a bit proud. Out of all the bookkeeping students, my books were those that were picked to be copied.

I was ready for a vacation when school was let out that spring even though it loomed long and lonely. My brother,

Loyal, was now in the Air Force stationed in Germany and Eleanor was staying with my brother, Herbert, in California. My friends all had summer jobs and I was without a boyfriend so I figured it would be a very boring summer.

Then a call came for me on my neighbor's telephone. Roy Dunn, the owner of the Dunvilla resort, was on the line offering me a summer job. I knew that some of my friends were working there so, without a thought to what my job would be, I said, "Yes!"

I threw some clothes in a bag and I was waiting when he drove into our driveway a short while later. When he told me, on the drive out, that I would be working behind the soda fountain, I got a pretty queasy feeling in the pit of my stomach. What had I gotten myself into?

I was put to work immediately and it took only one customer for me to realize that I couldn't handle it. When I was unable to hear what flavor of ice cream he wanted and I had to ask my partner, I was devastated. But I was determined that I would not return home. With the mutual agreement of my friend, Gen, who was the dishwasher, and with the consent of Mr. Dunn, we switched jobs.

Washing dishes certainly isn't as prestigious a job as a soda jerk, so I'm sure Mr. Dunn was taken by surprise but I didn't tell him my reason for changing. My job went off without a hitch and I got along well with the cook who had a reputation of being bossy, fussy and grumpy.

The summer I spent there, working and playing with my friends, was one of the highlights of my life. The check I received at the end of the season was used to buy some new school clothes. With the clothes and with a feeling of accomplishment, I began my senior year relaxed and with renewed confidence in myself.

AGAINST ALL ODDS

My hearing had gone from bad to worse by then so I knew what I was up against. The tools patience, humor, tolerance, self-esteem and perseverance would be used over and over.

I knew that if I had confided in my teachers, they would have helped make things easier for me. But now as I write, some things come to mind that make me think that most of them did know and, as inconspicuously as possible, tried to help me.

I remember during the oral spelling tests in English, Miss Serkland used the words in sentences and repeated the sentences as much as needed. Information, that I feel was not necessary, was written on the blackboards and when addressing me, teachers looked at me and spoke loud and clear.

But even so, I had to work extra hard and I became pretty good at creating innovative ideas to get me through some difficult times. Nowhere did I work harder in finding a solution to a problem than in my social studies class.

Our assignment, which would account for half of our final grade, was a 15-minute speech. I didn't especially look forward to getting up and speaking at a podium but I figured I could handle that. It was the questioning by my classmates after the speech that gave me the jitters. That was one time that I didn't volunteer to go first.

Day after day passed and I watched as one student after another gave a speech. I knew time was running out and if I didn't get up there, I would soon be called on. I was getting nervous and my mind was working overtime trying to figure a way out. Then I got a brilliant idea.

With a little over 15 minutes left in the period, I raised my hand and confidently walked up to the podium. I began to speak and I didn't stop until the bell rang, signaling the end of class. There wasn't time for any questions. I walked back to my desk, picked up my books and went on to my next class.

I was a bit apprehensive when I returned to class the next day. Would I have to return to the podium? I didn't. I may have fooled most of my classmates but I think Mr. Emmel was "on to me" and let me get away with it. He must have given me a good grade for my final grade was good.

I used the same tactics at Saturday morning confirmation class as I used in the classroom. I didn't wait for Pastor Jerstad to call on me. I volunteered an answer soon after the class began. If I waited, I soon found myself lost in a sea of chaos.

When the time for public questioning drew near, I became very apprehensive. I didn't know what I would do. I wouldn't be able to raise my hand then and furthermore, I wouldn't know what questions I would be asked. Other than remembering that I stood with my classmates in the aisle, that night is a total blank. I must have made it through as I was confirmed the following Sunday.

I think most kids are relieved when that part of their life is behind them and I was even more so. I still have to chuckle when I think of the time, many years later, when I had the privilege of attending service at a church in Minneapolis where Pastor Jerstad served after leaving Pelican Rapids. When I shook his hand and introduced my husband, he said, "Dora was one of my best students." I'm sure it was a line that he used over and over again.

From the grades on my report cards through the years, I figured I ranked in the top half of my class. But I didn't find out just where I ranked until many years after I graduated. As I filed by Mr. Martin, our superintendent, at the close of our last class meeting, he whispered my ranking in my ear and I wasn't able to hear it.

Me and Loyal—1953

It never was a concern of mine until I began to write *Journey Out of Silence*. Then my curiosity got the best of me. I wrote to Mr. Keith Klein, superintendent of the Pelican Rapids Schools for his help. At the same time, I asked him if he knew why I wasn't given special help.

A feeling of pride rippled through me when I read the words, "You graduated 18th from the top of a class of eighty-seven."

It was one battle I had won but I had many more to fight in the years following my graduation. Truly, I had been given a hard row to hoe but looking back, I know that I was given the strength to meet my challenges.

Another battle was just beginning at that time, the end of my senior year. Once again, inside my head something so frightening was happening that it was impossible for me to keep it to myself.

A few days before I was to graduate, I helped lay new linoleum in the dining room and then began to study for a final exam. When I began to read, I only saw half of what I focused on. I tried to tell Eleanor but what came out was "I can't wrote."

Then other things happened. One side of my body became numb and I began to see zigzag lines in my head. They started out small and grew bigger until that same side of my head was filled.

Me wearing my confirmation dress; our house in town—1952

Another fast trip was made to the clinic. The whole episode lasted about 20 minutes so by the time the doctor examined me, all the symptoms were gone, leaving me with no after effects. He told me that I may have had a mild stroke but no tests were done nor was I hospitalized.

My life continued on as though nothing had happened. I graduated and celebrated by sharing a sample bottle of Mogen David wine with my best friends, Avis and Betty.

Unknown to me, they had made plans to find jobs in Fargo and they left the week after graduation. I felt betrayed but I also knew my hearing loss would be an obstacle in finding a job working with the public. As to what my future held in store, I didn't have a clue.

Pelican Rapids Public Schools
Pelican Rapids, Minnesota 56572-0642

Keith Klein, Superintendent

August 20, 1997

Dear Mrs. Weber,

Enclosed you will find a transcript of your high school grades and also your class rank which indicates you graduated 18th from the top of a class of 87.

As far as your question is concerned relative as to why nothing was done to provide you special help with your hearing disability at that time, obviously, I have no answer. I can tell you, however, that great strides have been made in dealing with all students with learning disabilities and with hearing difficulties in particular.

We begin screening children for any disabilities even before they start school, usually at age four. If a disability is identified at that time, we provide special help even before this child enters kindergarten. The progress of the student is reviewed formally on an annual basis and modifications are made even more frequently if necessary.

For this upcoming school year, the Pelican Rapids School District has identified six students with some degree of hearing impairment which could affect their learning. To help these students, we employ a full-time teacher of the hearing impaired who will work with these students on an individual basis and monitor their progress.

I hope that this information is valuable to you and if I can be of further assistance, please do not hesitate to contact me.

Sincerely,

Keith Klein

Dora Tingelstad
English XI-II
January 7, 1955
(537 words)

Rain on the Roof

*"It's raining! It's pouring!
The old man is snoring!"*

Now, if that isn't the craziest saying I don't know what is! How do you suppose anything like snoring came to be associated with rain?

I'd sure like to see the night that I could snore away through a rain shower. That constant pitterpat of the raindrops against the roof gets to be quite monotonous. Not only is it monotonous but dangerous too! You can never tell when an over-sized drop is going to drill a hole right through the roof! You don't think so? Well, just wait and see.

I can't step out on the porch, while it's raining, for fear of being hit on the head and getting a brain concussion. How the parents of little tots dare let their children go gallivanting around in the rain is beyond me. It just goes to show how brainless people get as they grow older. You can't blame the poor kids for not knowing better 'cause as the saying goes, "Children follow in their parents footsteps."

Another thing which is hard to understand is how those wooden sticks with a round piece of cloth on the tip, I guess the people call them umbrellas, can possibly protect a person from rain. The only time I'd use one is while I was wearing a suit of armor. Those plastic raincoats you see people running around in aren't any better! I think stores would sell lots more if they were made of aluminum or steel. I'll jump for joy when that day comes!

My house is the only one in town that has iron bars on the outside of the windows. There's also another building down by the rive that has bars on its windows. Could be that they're for protection from rain too! I guess I'll have to look up the word "jail" sometime. I can't wait until some of my neighbors' windows break, so that I can get something back on some of those smart aleck people. they must think I'm "queer" or something 'cause they won't even come to visit me anymore. Secretly, I think those windows have broken but have been replaced while it was raining, so that they'd be shining again after the rain is over. Of course I wouldn't mention this to anyone.

I haven't always thought like this. It all started one day while I was listening to the radio. The announcer read a story that was written by the winner of the annual liars' contest. I have had many people call me a liar in my time, but I never did find out what it really meant. I just assumed that it meant something like "brilliant." Well, anyway the story went like this:

One day last summer, during a big rainstorm, a raindrop, as big as an egg, drilled a hole through the roof of my house, went through the floor of an upstairs bedroom, down through the floor of the kitchen and hit my dad, who was working in the basement, with such a force that he was unconscious for a couple of months afterwards.

Now, do you believe anything drastic can happen? What's that? Look up the word "Liar"?

Good and original. I like it. However, some of your sentences are rather cumbersome.

PART FOUR

GUIDING LIGHT

Of all the ear surgeries I underwent, that first one is still so memorable, it is as if it is etched on stone. I was awake under local anesthesia so my curiosity was given free rein. I looked all around the operating room and then up. A multitude of interns and students, all dressed in green scrubs, peered down at me from the observation deck. As the surgery progressed, I began to hear scraping and scratching sounds. Then Dr. Boies whispered in my ear. I wasn't able to hear immediately but with each attempt it became clearer.

Finally, I heard every wonderful word. The sweet something he whispered was, "You have beautiful red hair."

After hearing that, I thought my hair was okay but had it been purple, orange or green, I wouldn't have minded.

Good company on a journey, makes the way to seem the shorter.

Izaak Walton

There wasn't a telephone call with an offer of a job that summer and I did not have the courage to apply for one in town. Together with my sister, who had returned from California wearing a hearing aid that gave her confidence, I wrote letters of application to resorts in the area.

Nothing panned out. Either we didn't like the description of what our duties would be or our applications were rejected. We spent the summer loafing around the house waiting for the raspberries to ripen. Then, for a couple of weeks, we had jobs at a berry farm just north of town.

It was there, among the berry bushes with the hot July sun beating down on my head, that I experienced my second episode of zigzag lines dancing around in my head. That time I kept it to myself, picking my way right through it and, just as before, I was left without any after-effects.

When all the berries had been picked, I had a little money in my pocket but still I didn't have any plans for the future. I sometimes wonder just what my life would have been like if Mama had not intervened. She had grown weary of having two grown daughters underfoot and she justifiably gave us an ultimatum. Find a job or move out.

That was just what I needed—to be pushed out of the nest and to use my own wings. And it was to Hibbing, Minn. that I flew. My brother, LeRoy, and his wife Louella, opened their house and arms and invited Eleanor and me to stay with them while we searched for jobs.

I packed my clothes in my brand new luggage that I had received for graduation, used my berry-picking money for bus fare and boarded the Greyhound bus. That trip was the pivot point of my journey.

TO KNOW THEM WAS TO LOVE THEM

Eleanor began to look for a live-in domestic position but I wanted something different. It took only one interview for a sales clerk position at Woolworth's to show me just what I was up against.

I didn't have any problems filling out the application but the interview was a nightmare. I was so embarrassed when I wasn't able to understand that I had all I could do to contain myself. I wanted to just get up and leave long before it was finished. I knew then that I would not subject myself to another. I would do like my sister and look for a domestic job.

There was a major problem with that. In the whole town, only the Ian F. Scott Pearson family was advertising for help and Eleanor had already applied. Then she began to have misgivings and backed out.

The Pearson Family—1957
Anne, Jeanne, Grandma Pearson holding
Martha, Jim, Tom, Rob

It was a large family of five children with a baby expected in the fall. She didn't think she wanted that many in her charge so she decided not to take the job. Instead, she applied for a position in Minneapolis as a mother's helper for two children and was hired sight unseen.

She wanted me to go with her but I was adamant that I would not go. Just the thought of living in such a large city terrified me. When I went along with my brother when he took her down and I saw with my own eyes just how large it was, I was more sure than ever that I would never live there. I knew I couldn't stay with my brother forever so I decided to check out the family of seven plus one.

I fell in love with the big stucco house immediately. It was in a nice neighborhood with a park right across the street and downtown was within walking distance, a feature that very much appealed to me. Best of all, I liked Mrs. Pearson right away and I was very impressed with her husband's Scottish name, Ian F. Scott Pearson.

I was able to hear Mrs. Pearson easily so I didn't volunteer any information about my hearing loss. She explained to me what my duties would be, how much I would be paid and what days I would have off. She then showed me the private little room in the basement that would be mine and I was hired. I moved in the next morning.

Anne, Jim and Rob were in school when I arrived so I first became acquainted with Tom and Jeanne. And, oh, how cute they were. Tom, a husky little guy with a round little face, was four years old. Jeanne, who was two, was a petite girl with beautiful, long, blonde hair.

My first task was to supervise their afternoon baths before putting them down for their naps. Jeanne fell asleep in the security of her old pink thermal blanket while her brother fell asleep contentedly stroking a piece of a Playtex rubber pants, his thumb firmly stuck in his mouth.

It was a major catastrophe whenever Tom couldn't find that little piece of security. Then the house was turned upside down as the whole family searched for it. It was imperative that it was found as the stores no longer carried them and Mrs. Pearson had to special order them.

Rob was an older version of his little brother, Tom. He, too, was stocky and, oh, so very sweet. Jim, at age eight, was mature for his age and already very handsome.

When I first saw Anne, with her red hair and freckles, it was like seeing myself at ten years of age. As the months went by and she drew nearer to becoming a teen-ager, I could sense the turmoil that those years brought as I had experienced those same feelings only a few short years before. She would sometimes seek me out and confide in me and often times, when she was dressed up for Sunday morning church service, she would come to me for approval. All five children got along well with one another and they were a joy to be with. As hard as I try, I cannot remember one instance of fighting among them.

Mr. Pearson, a tall, distinguished-looking man, had his own accounting firm. What I remember the most about him was that it was his responsibility to see that his family began the day with a nourishing breakfast.

I can't recall what he fixed on other mornings but Friday was always soup day. The first Friday, when I came into the kitchen and saw what he was fixing, I wondered if he would dish up some for me. He did and I had no choice but to eat it. And, oh, how good it tasted. After that, I always looked forward to Friday and soup day. He fixed many different kinds but I was always the happiest when I found split green pea in my bowl.

After only a short while, the responsibility of preparing lunch and dinner was given to me. I certainly didn't bring any experience in cooking along from home but the training I had received in Home Economics class came in very handy.

The family sat down to many dinners of twice-baked potatoes and broiled meatballs wrapped in a slice of bacon. I still add a can of vegetable beef soup to my meatballs, a trick that Mr. Pearson's mother showed me when she visited from Scotland.

Open-faced broiled tuna sandwiches were a favorite of all the kids and I made them often for lunch. I made many double batches of cookies and dreambars and large bowls of Jell-O soufflé, a whipped strawberry Jell-O, Carnation Milk dessert.

The heavy cleaning and ironing were left to the cleaning and ironing ladies that Mrs. Pearson employed. But Saturday mornings I went from room to room changing sheets on the many beds. I learned how to make hospital style square corners and to make the weekly laundry lighter, the top sheet was moved to the bottom and only the bottom sheet was put in the wash.

I also became familiar with the use of an automatic dishwasher and a garbage disposal. Both were luxuries to me and made washing dishes a snap; that is, if I put the right amount of soap in. If not, the suds would squeeze out of the sides and over the top. The kitchen floor would be flooded and I would be called back up from my room to help Mr. Pearson swab the deck.

I was very naive when I arrived at the Pearsons so I look on the years that I spent with them as a training period. I was even given training in the care of a newborn baby when little Martha was born. She was entrusted into my care when she was only two weeks old.

That Sunday morning when I came upstairs, the family was dressed and ready to go to church. Mrs. Pearson came into the living room carrying Martha. Mr. Pearson followed close behind with a bottle in his hand. Martha was placed in my arms and I was handed the bottle. After a quick lesson on feeding and burping a baby, we were left alone.

I was nervous and I'm sure Mrs. Pearson was even more so. I wonder if she was able to concentrate on the sermon that morning. But when they came home, Martha was sound asleep in her crib. From that day on, she was my "afternoon baby."

Mrs. Pearson cared for Martha in the mornings while I did the list of chores that she had for me each day. Then after my rest period and Martha's nap, she was mine for the afternoon. I was given permission to dress her in any of her pretty little dresses and to entertain her in any way I chose. Usually I put her in her buggy and we walked to the corner grocery store to pick up something that was needed for supper. But more times than not, I proudly pushed her around the neighborhood or sat in the park, all the while pretending that she was mine.

MRS. PEARSON'S DREAM BARS

½ C. butter
1 C. all-purpose flour
½ C. brown sugar

Blend with a pastry blender or fingertips as for pie crust. Press or pat in buttered pan. Bake until light brown, about 10 min., in moderate oven.

1 C. brown sugar
2 eggs
2 Tbls. all-purpose flour
¼ tsp. baking soda
pinch of salt
½ tsp. vanilla
1 ½ C. coconut
1 C. nuts

Beat eggs. Add brown sugar. Now add flour, soda and salt which have been well mixed. Fold in vanilla, nuts and coconut. Place mixture on top of first mixture and spread. Bake for 20 min. at 325°. Cool and cut into squares.

Picnic with the Pound Family
Janet, me, Ted, Hattie, and Jim—1958

Grandma Pearson's Scotch Eggs

Hard boil required number of eggs. Remove shells. Skin sausages (one for each egg) and mold around each egg, covering it all. Dip in beaten egg and then into cracker crumbs or "old-fashioned" bread crumbs. Fry in hot oil for 3-5 minutes.

First Love—A Tribute to Bill

Wednesday was my day off and I was free to leave after washing the breakfast dishes; then I hurried to get dressed. Before I left, I had a meeting with Mrs. Pearson in the dining room where we had a little conference. We would discuss the past week and future changes and then I would get my week's wages.

Seventeen dollars and fifty cents seemed like a lot of money back then and I was very frugal. Instead of purchasing ready-made clothing, I bought fabric and sewed my own clothes with the machine that Mrs. Pearson let me use. Because I didn't yet have any friends to do things with, I was even able to save money in the form of U.S. Savings Bonds.

My days off were spent with either my brother LeRoy's or my brother Alvin's families. Even after spending six days with the Pearson children, I had enough love to lavish on my nieces Linda and Diane and nephews Steven and Jerry. Although I loved them equally, I'm afraid that more time was spent with LeRoy's family—for a very good reason. My sister-in-law's brother Bill might be there.

I had seen Bill several times before I moved to Hibbing and we had such a good time together. He was always so cheerful and kind. But what drew me to him the most was that he had grown up with a disability and he, too, had overcome it.

When he was only eighteen months old, the car in which he was riding was hit by a train. An older brother was killed and Bill's right arm was severed below the elbow.

Over the years, he had become so proficient that there was little that those with two arms could do better than he could. I always marveled at how easily he accomplished what he set out to do. Even tying his shoes looked so easy. Those were the initial qualities that drew me towards him but soon I began to be drawn to him in a more personal way.

He was so thoughtful and considerate of others. He was dependable and he had a terrific sense of humor. When he began "showing off" for me and teasing me, I loved it. I also loved his loud and unpretentious family which took me under their wings and treated me like their own.

I was included in most of their family gatherings and I was always on the lookout for Bill. If he wasn't there, I was let down but if he walked in the door, I would light up like a Christmas tree. Anyone would have had to be blind not to notice the effect that he had on me. The more I was included in the family gatherings, the more we were thrown together.

He began to call me during the week just to chat and then he finally asked me for a date—but not one alone with him yet. Our first dates were bowling dates in the company of his family, first at the bowling lanes in Hibbing and then at the lanes in surrounding towns. Those little trips were special in themselves.

Bill liked country western music as well as I did and I found out that he and his dad also liked to sing. They serenaded me with song after song and I just knew that Bill was singing only to me.

During the week, when I was back in my room, I would lay on my bed and tune my radio to the country western station. I wanted to learn the words of the songs, too. But to hear well enough, I would have to turn the volume up. Often, I would fall asleep and wake up to find that Mrs. Pearson had come down and turned the radio off. Maybe that was when she made the decision to do something about my hearing.

ETCHED ON STONE

I don't have any recollections of Dr. L.W. Morsman, the ear specialist Mrs. Pearson took me to see but I do remember his office and his mode of testing very well.

He had a very small office and the testing was done in a very unconventional manner. He was both my audiologist and my audiometer. He spoke to me with his voice in various pitches all the while positioning me in various spots around his office.

When the testing was done, I found out that my type of hearing loss actually had a name, *otosclerosis,* and that I had inherited it from Mama. I also found out that the noise in my head had a name, *tinnitus,* and that it was caused by the otosclerosis. I walked out of Dr. Morsman's office sporting a hearing aid in my right ear and with a heart filled with hope.

Dr. Morsman told me that a procedure called a stapes mobilization was just beginning to be used at the University of Minnesota to correct the hearing loss caused by otosclerosis and he referred me to Dr. Lawrence R. Boies, Sr. I certainly wasn't expecting to hear what my brother, LeRoy, told me when I asked him if he would take me.

He, too, was losing his hearing and also wanted to find out if the stapes mobilization would help him. It was a complete surprise to learn that he couldn't hear well and, once again, I give the credit to the environment at home and also to that of his in-laws.

On August 12, 1957, a few days before our birthdays, we walked into the University Hospital, which is now the Mayo Building, and went in search of the Department of Otolaryngology. There, for the first of many, many times, I stepped up into a sound-proof booth and struggled to hear the sounds through the cumbersome set of earphones that was strapped over my head.

I will always remember Dr. Lawrence R. Boies, Sr. He was a short man with a big smile and a heart filled with love. I knew immediately that I was important to him, not as a patient but as a teen-aged girl whose hearing he hoped to restore.

LeRoy and I were accepted for surgery and we were admitted to the hospital that evening. Our surgeries were scheduled for early in the morning. LeRoy was to go first and I would follow shortly after.

Of all the ear surgeries I underwent, that first one is still so memorable, it is as if it was etched on stone. I was awake under local anesthesia so my curiosity was given free rein. I looked all around the operating room and then up. A multitude of interns and students, all dressed in green scrubs, peered down at me from the observation deck.

As the surgery progressed, I began to hear scraping and scratching sounds. Then Dr. Boies whispered in my ear. I wasn't able to hear immediately but with each attempt, it became clearer.

Finally, I was able to hear every wonderful word. The sweet something that he whispered was, "You have beautiful red hair."

After hearing that, I thought my hair was OK but had it been purple, orange or green, I wouldn't have minded.

I can still see Dr. Boies smiling down at me and feel the pressure of his hand when he squeezed my shoulder reassuringly as I was wheeled out of the operating room.

I was very dizzy after surgery and I laid on the back seat of the car during the trip back to Hibbing. I remember wondering how LeRoy was able to drive but it was a long time before I found out.

His surgery was unsuccessful and he had undergone it knowing that the odds were against him having any improvement. He didn't think I would have had the surgery if he didn't so he put my welfare ahead of his. I am deeply grateful for that and I thank him but I don't think he knew me as well as he thought he did. I know that I would have gone through it even if they had left me there alone.

A month later, I had enough confidence in myself to take the Greyhound bus to Minneapolis for my first check-up. Once again, I was ushered into the sound-proof booth. On my records, Dr. Boies wrote, "Has some improvement—wishes to try the other ear (I will arrange it) ." On a return visit six months later, he wrote, "Has a distinct improvement." More than a year would pass before I would return to try the other ear.

The winter after I had my stapes mobilization surgery, another member of my family had it done—my sister, Eleanor. Unfortunately, like LeRoy's, her surgery was unsuccessful.

RESTLESS MOMENTS

There wasn't a dramatic change in my hearing and I soon was back to using my hearing aid. It was easier to talk to others both in person and by telephone and I could hear the telephone ring from any room in the house. I'm sure, too, that Mrs. Pearson was relieved I no longer had to have the volume of the radio up so loud and she must have been more comfortable when she left her family in my care. I'm sure it made life easier for Bill as he, too, was undergoing a change in his life at the same time.

A benefactor was so impressed with his cheerfulness and the way he handled his job as a bell-hop at the Androy Hotel that he wanted to make Bill's job easier. The benefactor bought him a prosthesis.

Bill did give it a fighting chance but because he had become so proficient with only one arm, the prosthesis was more of a hindrance than anything else. It was especially awkward when we were on a date and very often it came between us. To put it simply, I did not like being hugged by a robot. I much preferred to be held in the softness of his arms.

Actually, we made quite a comely couple, he with his prosthesis and me with my hearing aid. More often than not, his prosthesis ended up in the back seat of his car and many a romantic moment was spoiled by the incessant "beeeeep" of my hearing aid.

I don't really know when I began to feel restless or why. Probably it was just time to get on with my journey. Oh, I still loved the Pearson family dearly but something that Mrs. Pearson had not reckoned with was that I became dissatisfied with my job and I could not visualize staying there forever. When the chance came for me to move to California, I took it.

LeRoy and his family were going to take a trip to visit my brother Herbert's family and they invited Eleanor and me to go along. We could stay there and look for jobs. California had always seemed to me to be so magical and glamorous and now I would have the chance to live there.

The night before I left, Bill and I sat in his car and talked into the early morning. Neither of us were ready to make a commitment. Bill had the same dream that I once had of being a teacher. I didn't know yet what I wanted but I knew that it wasn't as a domestic. I wanted my independence and I was confident that I would find it in sunny California.

Bill did go on to pursue his dream. He graduated from Bemidji State Teacher's College and taught at the Rainy River Community College in International Falls, Minn. He married a girl named Elnora and they were blessed with three daughters. I frequently saw Bill and his family until cancer took his life at the young age of 55.

Although the Pearson family was never far from my mind and I frequently had dreams of returning to them, I lost contact with them when I moved to California. They had been such an important stopover on my journey that when I began to write, I knew I wanted to see them once again. Forty years had passed since I left so I knew that, if they were still living, Mr. and Mrs. Pearson would be near eighty years old. I took my chances.

I wrote a letter, addressed to the Ian F. Scott Pearson family and sent it on its way to the Hibbing, Minn. postmaster. The letter came back marked "Undeliverable" but along with it, the postmaster sent a copy of the Pearson names taken from the telephone book. Ian F. Scott was not among the list.

I wrote a form letter to two James', two Thomas' and one Robert. All James' and Thomas' letters were returned.

Several weeks went by without an answer from Robert and I had given up hope of ever seeing any of them again. Then one day when I came home after a day at the University of Minnesota Hospital, there was a message on our telephone from Anne Pearson Gerber and in the mail was a letter from Rob.

After reading Rob's letter, my emotions were in such turmoil that I could not return Anne's call until the following day. Much to my surprise, Anne, Tom, Jeanne and Martha all live in the Twin Cities and I was so very happy to hear that Mrs. Pearson, at 80, is well and also living near me. Jim lives in California and Rob is holding down the fort in Hibbing.

On February 7, 1998, I was reunited with Mrs. Pearson and Anne. We spent several hours reminiscing. I cannot say we got to know one another again as none of us is the same as we were forty years ago. The one question I wanted answered the most was why Mrs. Pearson took it upon herself to seek help for my hearing loss.

She said, "We were very fond of you and, at the same time, we were concerned for the welfare of our children."

There could not have been any better reasons. She could not remember my country western music blaring from the radio

Only a Dream

My dream of a sunny California turned out to be just that, a dream. Not only was the weather dreary all the while I was there, the chance of finding a job was also.

I did keep my resolution, though, and I began my search within a few days of my arrival. First, I applied to be a switchboard operator at the telephone company but I wasn't hired—and for a good reason. I couldn't hear without my hearing aid and I couldn't wear the head-set over the hearing aid.

Me—1958

Don—1958

My next try was at Travis Air Force Base where I spent a day undergoing a battery of Civil Service exams. I didn't have any problems there. I was able to hear the instructions well and I whizzed through all parts of the exams. The only problem was that it would take several weeks before I found out the results and I was running out of money. To bide my time, I decided to once again get a job as a mother's helper.

I had two interviews. The one I chose was to care for the children of a single mom. I stayed only one day. The conditions were so dreadful that I could not return the following day.

By then, Christmas was fast approaching and I was lonesome. I found out first hand just how true the saying, "You don't miss someone until they're taken away" really is. I missed the Pearson family but I especially missed Bill. I was too stubborn to write to either. Even the letter I received from Mrs. Pearson, with an offer to help me attend Junior College, couldn't entice me to return. I would not admit that my dream of finding the good life in California had failed.

I had made up my mind to return to Minnesota. Not even the passing grade on the Civil Service exam with the appointment for an interview could change my mind.

A few days before Christmas, Eleanor and I once again boarded a Greyhound bus. It was a much longer trip that time and it brought us right back to where we had started almost three years earlier.

LONESOME ONCE MORE

There wasn't a band to welcome us home nor was a red carpet laid out for us. But that didn't matter as we didn't linger there for long. Eleanor got her old job back in Minneapolis and that time I went, too. I was hired for a similar position for the family who lived just across the street.

The work wasn't near as strenuous as it had been at Pearson's but caring for the six Pearson children had been a great deal more pleasant than my two new charges. By springtime, I was looking for a new position.

I found one as a nanny for the two children of Mr. and Mrs. Stewart of the Stewart Lumber Co. I got along well with the children but there was a personality conflict between Mrs. Stewart and me from the very beginning and I accept the blame. I just was no longer content to clean someone else's home or to care for someone else's children. I wanted my own home and children and I came very close to getting them even though my instincts, once again, told me "No."

Remember Don, the first boy I went steady with? Mutual friends got us back together again. He was in the Air Force and stationed in St. Charles, Louisiana. We began to correspond

*Friends at Trabert Hall
Red, Eleanor, Karen and me—1958*

and soon, out of mutual loneliness, we were making plans to be married when he came home on his next leave.

I gave my notice to Mrs. Stewart and a week before he was to arrive, I packed my suitcases once more and went home to Pelican Rapids to wait for him. I waited and I waited but he did not come. I remember being a bit apprehensive but I felt no remorse. Instead, just as I had done when he broke up with me in high school, I felt relieved. I never received a letter of explanation from him but, not long after, I heard that he had met and married someone else when he was on that very same leave.

So it was back to Minneapolis once again. This time it was under completely different circumstances. Eleanor, too, had become disenchanted with her domestic job and had moved into Trabert Hall, a rooming house for girls like us. I moved in with her and we began our search for employment, a search that began with several visits to the Minnesota State Employment Office where we took aptitude tests.

Just as they did in high school, the tests pointed me towards a career in engineering and also showed that I had excellent manual dexterity. I can understand how my manual dexterity helped me get my first job folding diapers at the Crib Diaper Co. It's the engineering that puzzles me unless it helped me place the diapers in neat, systematic piles.

That job wasn't any more prestigious than my job as dishwasher at Dunvilla but I was proud to be on my own. I wasn't alone. Eleanor was working there, too, just around the corner in the laundry. It was a fun job as I was surrounded by a group of very diverse co-workers.

There was the German speaking girl whose agenda it was to always fold the most bundles. There was Evelyn who dressed up as if she was working in an office and Dorie who was so soft-hearted that not many days went by without her crying on Marge's shoulder, the mother to all of us.

And there was Richard, the only male among all us ladies. He was my first date in the city, a double date with his friends to tour the State Capitol Building on a Sunday afternoon. It was a date that didn't get off to a very good start.

Just as I got into the car, I heard the siren of a police car. I very smartly said, "They're coming after us before we get started." Oh, it was a smart remark all right. So smart, in fact, that the other girl had beat me to it. The day was spoiled. I had one more date with him before he left for military service. I left soon after. It was time to get on with my journey.

My next job was at the Paul Bunyan Bait Co. where I assembled everything except fishing baits. I put handles on hunting and recreational bows, feathers on arrows and made all kinds of fishing rods, from deep sea to fly rods. Not only did I enjoy my job but there was an increase in my salary.

Eleanor found a more interesting and better paying job as a lettering designer at a shirt company. Together with two friends, we moved into our own apartment.

That was the beginning of a whole new social life for me. There was an ample number of young men and only one other young girl working at the factory and she was engaged. It didn't take long for me to find out that I actually did appeal to the opposite sex.

With the help of "Shen," who became my surrogate father, I was first approached by Don. We went out a few times and although I thought he was very nice, our relationship didn't get beyond the friendship stage. There was one obstacle I couldn't overcome. I was so much taller than he. I'm sure I didn't break his heart. I introduced him to my roommate and they were married soon after.

Me and Joe—1959
In Eleanor's and my first apartment

I dated a few guys after that but none interested me until my new foreman, Joe, came on the scene. He was tall, dark and handsome, the man of my dreams and he was interested in me! He began giving me a ride home in his sleek, new sports car and soon, against fair warning from "Shen," I had fallen for him hook, line and sinker.

One morning when I came to work, rumors were running rampant and everyone made sure that I knew. Joe was in his office with a girl and she was wearing a diamond ring.

Oh, he tried to explain his way out but I turned my deaf ear to him. Once again, I decided that it was time to move on. Before I did, there was something else I had to do. Once more, my hearing had begun to deteriorate and I needed to see Dr. Boies.

No Improvement

I don't think Dr. Boies was near as willing to do a stapes mobi-lization on my right ear as he was on my left. But my persis-tence won out.

On the report of that April 21, 1959 visit, he wrote, "Patient insists that her left ear is better—wants the right one done. I will do the right ear at the patient's request."

One month later, on May 25, I once again was admitted to the University of Minnesota Hospital. My arrival and departure are the only things I remember of that visit. I was not yet 21 years old so my sister was waiting to give permission. I left the hospital alone.

I caught the city bus outside the hospital and rode the waves of euphoria all the way to my apartment thinking that I could hear better. That lasted right up until my return visit on June 18. Then I heard Dr. Boies tell me, "No improvement."

Life went on. With the encouragement of a friend, I applied for a job as a file clerk at the Great Northern Insurance Company, an insurer of automobiles, the same place my friend worked. The interview with George V. Plaster, company presi-dent, went well.

The decision to tell him that I wore a hearing aid was the right decision but I didn't know it then. I wasn't hired on the spot. He first wanted to check out my high school grades. He told me he would call me that weekend. I stuck close to the telephone.

When I had not yet heard from him by Sunday afternoon, I had all but given up hope and when the telephone rang late that night, I certainly didn't expect it to be him. But it was and all the math classes I had taken in high school had added up. I wasn't hired to be a file clerk; I was hired as a rate clerk.

I loved the lifestyle of working in an office downtown. After having worn slacks for so long, my wardrobe didn't contain many dress clothes so with the increase in my salary, I was able to buy some career clothes. I even bought some high heels and I began to splurge on permanents and haircuts at the beauty salon. I also began to window shop, looking at the new models of hearing aids.

I was still wearing my first one. Although it did help me hear better, it was ill-fitting with an ear mold that was not custom made. I could no longer turn the volume up as loud as I needed without getting the noisy "feedback." I had to be careful, too, for if I turned my head too rapidly or bumped it, the hearing aid fell out of my ear.

I decided I had done enough window shopping and I walked into Telex Hearing Center, a dealership I passed every day on my way to work. My visit there was the first of many such visits to various dealers I would experience over the next twenty-five years. They ran the gambit from poor to excellent. Telex Hearing Aid Center was excellent. Everything was handled in a professional and caring manner by experienced salespeople.

My hearing was tested and I was counseled about the advantages of binaural (both ears) hearing aids. Molds were made for the ear molds that I would need for the two-ear hearing aids that I ordered. And, oh, they were right about the benefits of binaural aids. A new world was opened up to me the day they were placed in my ears.

I was then able to relax and really get to know my Co-workers. As I did so, I discovered that, like me, several others had disabilities, some mental and some physical. I wondered why. That was one more question I wanted answered when I began to write about my journey. Did it just happen to be that way or was it planned? Thirty-seven years had passed but that did not deter me from trying to find out. I would try to contact Mr. Plaster.

I took out the telephone directory and ran my finger down the column of Plasters and there it was, "George V. Plaster." I wrote a letter.

Weeks went by, and just as I had done when I didn't get an answer from the Pearsons, I gave up hope of hearing from him. But it did come. Not written by George but a lovely letter written by his wife Virginia. She wrote:

Monday, 11-3-97

Dear Dora,

I'm sorry this is late for you but I have had a few problems such as a concussion that I've been dealing with and not able to do all I want to do.

Thank you for the nice letter that you sent to George. I'm sorry but he passed away 6 yrs. ago after 3 strokes.

Yes he was a very kind and caring person and I remember his telling me about hiring persons that some others didn't agree with but he felt he knew better. His brother was cerebral palsy and all his life he had cared for him and knew too that Philip with some training could do many things.

Happy to hear of your happy life and 4 sons—we had 2 sons—and your surgery that went so well—keep up the good work.

Sorry again I couldn't help any more and George would feel pleased that you thought of him—hope your research goes well.

Sincerely,

Virginia Plaster

What an honor it was for me to have worked for a man such as George Plaster, one who didn't wait for the American Disability Act to be passed. Against opposition, he had the courage and faith to hire me and others with disabilities. I am confident that I did not let him down as two other girls wearing hearing aids were hired while I still worked there.

THE UNVEILING

The improvement in my hearing that binaural hearing aids gave me also helped make me less self-conscious about wearing a hearing aid. I no longer was concerned if others found out but I still thought they were ugly so I wore my hair long and was careful that my ears were always covered. So when I saw the model of eyeglasses with the aids concealed in the bows, I didn't waste time ordering a pair.

I had my hair cut and had a stylish Afro permanent that covered the ear molds nicely. It didn't take me long to discover that covering my earmolds was the only advantage of these eyeglasses.

In winter or summer, when the lenses of my glasses fogged up, I had to take my hearing aids off right along with my glasses. If they got dirty or rain splattered on them, off my aids had to come. If I took a nap during the day and wanted to be aware of what was going on around me, I had to sleep with my glasses on. But the biggest disadvantage to wearing them was when I was on a date.

I didn't volunteer the information that I wore hearing aids to my dates until we became better acquainted. So when I began to wear my new aids, it was very easy to conceal them. But what would my explanation be when they took me home at the end of a date and they expected me to take my glasses off?

It was a no-win solution. If I took them off, I wasn't able to hear him but, if I left them on, I was thought to be a prude. I didn't wait for those aids to wear out. In no time at all, I was once again wearing over- the-ear models.

Myron—1961

The experiences I had with Don and Joe hadn't left me with negative feelings about guys but it did cause me to be more careful. I had several boyfriends after Joe. Some broke up with me and I broke up with some. Maybe I had become too fussy as eventually I found myself without any.

My girl friends were all going steady or were engaged and I didn't have anyone to go with me to where the boys were. Then, too, my fifth-year class reunion was getting close and my best friends, Avis and Betty, were married. I began to think I would never date another guy again. But, of course, I did and he had never been far from me.

When our old television went on the blink, my roommate's boyfriend had just the right repairman to come over to fix it— his roommate. As payment for his work, I fixed supper for him the following evening. I don't know if he liked me or my cooking.

Perhaps you can decide. This is the recipe for the casserole I made that evening.

PORK CHOP SPAGHETTI CASSEROLE

½ of 8-oz. pkg. of spaghetti, broken into pieces
4 pork chops
2 T. butter
1 T. flour
1 C. milk
¾ t. salt
¼ t. pepper
1 C. shredded sharp American cheese
1 #2 can whole tomatoes
salt and pepper

Preheat oven to 350°. Cook spaghetti in boiling salt water. Brown chops 10 min. on each side. Melt butter in saucepan, stir in flour. Turn heat to low. Add milk gradually, stirring constantly. Cook until mixture thickens. Add cheese and stir until it melts. Blend in tomatoes. Combine sauce and spaghetti in casserole dish. Place chops on top. Cover and bake 30 min. Uncover and bake 15 min. longer. Serves 4.

Whether it was me or my cooking, he asked me to go bowling with him that weekend. We hit it off well and soon we were going steady.

As I think back on these five years of my journey, I can see the light that so brightly guided me along the way. There were so many standing along the side of the road to help me. From one to another I went—from my brother, LeRoy, to Mrs. Pearson; from Dr. Morsman to Dr. Lawrence R. Boies, Sr. to George V. Plaster.

And then, at long last, I was placed in the loving arms of Myron, the guy I would share the rest of my life with.

PART FIVE

I'LL LOVE HIM FOREVER

If our marriage had been made in heaven, we certainly didn't think so then. From the very beginning we were plagued with debts. If Myron had thought that two could live as cheaply as one, he was very disillusioned. He came into our marriage debt free, without even a car payment.

I had plenty of debts. I was still paying for my last stapes mobilization surgery and I had a big, fat payment book for my hearing aids. Then, before the ink had time to dry on our wedding certificate, I discovered I was pregnant.

There is no more lovely, friendly and charming relationship, or company than a good marriage.

Martin Luther

Myron and I celebrated our thirty-seventh wedding anniversary this past winter. When our son, Kenny, and his family came over with good wishes, our daughter-in-law, Janine, asked us, "What did you do on your dates?"

Then, before we could answer her, she looked at me and asked, "Did you do most of the talking?"

That made me laugh and I was surprised, too, to know that in the four years she and Kenny have been married, she has come to know me well.

Actually, talking was never a problem for us. Quite possibly, that is what kept us together the first few weeks after we met for we had a problem much greater than that. We had so little in common that the adage, "Opposites attract," could very well have been penned for us.

We didn't like the same kind of movies and we didn't like the same type of music. Myron was a diehard fan of old war movies, westerns and science fiction while I preferred a musical or a good old-fashioned love story. He liked popular music and The Tijuana Brass and I liked the country-western music of Johnny Cash, Hank Williams and Eddie Arnold. While I liked to dance, something that was as much a part of me as my red hair, he was content to just sit and listen to the music.

Oh, he was a good sport and he did try to learn but he was so uncoordinated that as long and as hard as I tried, the best I could get out of him was a slow back and forth shuffle.

It was a different scene in a bowling alley, though. He was right at home there and what he lacked on the dance floor, he more than made up for on the bowling alley. He was a terrific bowler and he proved to be a better teacher than I. He helped me improve my game so much that I joined a bowling league. It wasn't long after that we began participating, though not too successfully, in mixed double tournaments.

We do have one thing in common and it has remained a constant throughout our marriage. We both love sports, especially basketball and especially the Minnesota Gopher Basketball Team. But circumstances, beyond my control, kept us from enjoying the games together. Myron and his friend, Bob, bought season tickets before I came on the scene so on game nights, I was left grudgingly behind.

I would be remiss if I didn't mention Myron's new, shiny black Ford and I would not be totally honest if I didn't admit that it endeared him to me. After riding in the cars of other guys which barely held together, I felt like Cinderella must have felt while riding in her coach. It was every bit as enchanting as it became the setting from which fairy tales are made.

We ate many an order of French fries and hamburgers while we sat in the parking lot of the Sun Drive-in, located in North Minneapolis. We took many Sunday drives to Chaska and the surrounding countryside where Myron had grown up. He showed me the house in town where he had lived with his grandparents when he was in high school and the farm where he had lived as a little boy.

It was then, while driving down an old country road, that he had me believing he was a romantic at heart. When he stopped the car alongside a grove of trees and told me he was going to go look for a "special" tree, I thought, *Oh, my, he's going to carve our initials on it.*

That wasn't what was on his mind. He wanted to see if he could find a dime he had once stuck under the bark when he was out hunting. When he came back to the car, there was a grin a mile wide on his face so I knew he had found it.

Over the years he forgot about that dime but if the tree is still there, so is the dime and I have never forgotten it. It is much more than just a dime to me. It is a symbol of the trust and confidence Myron had in me for sharing what to him was something very special.

Our relationship deepened after that. Two weeks later, when we were once again parked alongside those trees, he asked me to go steady. That time I didn't go against my instincts. I did what my heart told me to do, I said "Yes," and I became the proud recipient of another big class ring that needed to have tape wound around it.

I didn't have to change the tape once as only three weeks later, once again out in the country, Myron surprised me by asking me to marry him.

Again, I listened to my instincts and said, "Yes." Two weeks later, this time parked outside my apartment on First Avenue South, Myron took his class ring off my finger and replaced it with the sparkling diamond ring that still sparkles just as brightly today.

I PLEDGE THEE MY TROSS

We got a lot of razzing when we told our friends we were going to be married that winter. If we had been given a dollar for every time we were asked, "Was it getting too cold in the car?" we would have had enough money to pay for our wedding.

Myron wore a long tweed overcoat that had sleeves wide enough to accommodate my arms, too, so I don't remember being cold but a lot of gas was used up while the car idled so maybe the winter did rush us along. Anyway, we set the date for February 4, giving us only one month in which to get ready.

But before we did that, we had a little discussion about how big our family should be. Of course, we didn't agree on that, either. Myron was an only child and he thought that had been just fine so if we had only one child, that was OK with him.

Not so with me. Like Mama, I loved babies and I could have had a dozen but I told him I wanted four. No way! So we compromised and met halfway but secretly, I figured that one way or another, I would get those other two.

Then there was the matter of meeting our future in-laws and relatives. My family welcomed Myron with open arms when I took him to meet them. After he told me that I would fit right into his family because I was a lot like his aunts, I wasn't too worried about being accepted by his mother and grandparents. What worried me more was that I wouldn't be able to hear them.

I had it all wrong. Grandma only spoke German and Grandpa spoke broken English so even if I had been able to hear them, I wouldn't have understood them.

Myron's mother did speak quietly but I was able to hear her. It was her close scrutiny of me that I wasn't prepared for. It made me very ill-at-ease and uncharacteristically quiet. But maybe the first wrong impression that they got of me worked in my favor for Myron's mother was the epitome, and I don't mean it in a derogatory way, of the 3 P's—prim, proud and proper.

I'm sure, too, that being brought up in the Lutheran faith was in my favor. Since Myron was a member of St. John's in Chaska, they thought we should have our wedding there.

Not me. I didn't want any of the pomp and circumstance that went with a church wedding. What I wanted was much easier—to tie the knot in the pastor's study but I kept my wishes to myself and got busy making plans.

With only one month in which to get everything organized, I was kept busy but at night the fear would creep in. By the time of the Friday night practice, I was a nervous wreck. The same frightening feeling that I had on the ride out to my first job hit me full force as we drove to Chaska and, like then, I wondered, *What am I getting myself into?*

If I couldn't hear Pastor Kohn well enough to be able to repeat my vows, would I be able to bluff my way through? If I didn't say them correctly, would I be legally married? Or worse still, would I embarrass Myron so badly that he would leave me standing at the altar?

Well, I did have to resort to a bit of bluffing but not until the very last word. Everything came through loud and clear until I was to repeat, "Therefore, I pledge thee my troth." What I pledged to Myron that night was my "tross."

Myron and me on our Wedding Day—February 4, 1961

Right up until the wedding ceremony, I wondered what my tross was but I was too embarrassed to ask anyone. I really didn't think I had heard correctly but if that was the only mistake, I figured it wasn't too bad. But on Saturday, I was perfect! I heard, "Therefore I pledge thee my troth."

I never did bother to find out, until recently, what Myron would have gotten if I had pledged him my tross. I looked it up in the dictionary but it was not there. Good thing I heard right or he would not have received anything from me.

After a weekend honeymoon, we moved into a furnished basement apartment in a private home out in the boondocks of Bloomington, Minn. From all outward appearances, we thought we had found the perfect little love nest but it turned out to be a hornet's nest. It was so damp that it left our clothing smelling of mildew and if we left our shoes on the floor overnight, we stepped into soggy shoes in the morning. The kitchen sink was always getting plugged up, the washing machine only worked when it felt like it and we were always under the watchful eyes of our landlords.

Those were only minor inconveniences. We had a much more serious problem. If our marriage had been made in heaven, we certainly didn't think so then. From the very beginning we were plagued with debts. If Myron had thought that two could live as cheaply as one, he was very disillusioned. He came into our marriage debt free, without even a car payment.

I had plenty of debts. I was still paying for my last stapes mobilization surgery and I had a big, fat payment book for my hearing aids. Then, before the ink had time to dry on our wedding certificate, I discovered I was pregnant.

Then, to make matters even worse, when our landlords found out that a baby was on the way, we were told, "No babies allowed." We had to go apartment hunting again. This time we moved into a furnished upstairs apartment in an old converted home in South Minneapolis that was much nearer to downtown.

I had a very easy pregnancy once Myron stopped wanting me to cook, not like his mother, but his grandmother. I put up with the rabbit and ducks but when he began to bring fish home, head and all, I couldn't stomach it. I finally told him that if he wanted someone to cook like that, it would have to be Grandma, not me.

He relented and stopped bringing rabbit and duck home. The fish, although I still didn't care to fix it, at least came into the kitchen beheaded and ready for the frying pan.

My plans were to continue working right up until the time of our baby's birth but I caught a virus in August that landed me in the hospital. I did return when I was well but it was an uphill battle after that. I gave up and stayed home, leaving everything to fall on Myron's shoulders.

Luckily for us, Hennepin Transportation, the trucking company he was working for, was sold to Bruce Motor Freight and he began working in the office there. He liked his job much better and the increase in his salary, along with a better health insurance plan, went a long way in making life a bit easier for him.

AND BABY MAKES THREE

Charles Myron was born on November 28, 1961. He made sure that I knew he was coming. After twelve hours of grueling labor, I understood why. Like his mother, he was almost 10 pounds and he, too, had red hair. When I held him for the first time and told him he was a beautiful little baby, he must have wondered, *How can a 10 pound baby with red hair be little and beautiful?* But he was and he was such a good-natured little guy and besides he was all mine.

We had been home for only a few days when I found out why Myron only wanted one child. It wasn't that he didn't like babies, he was afraid of them. He was as uncoordinated when holding Chuck as he was on the dance floor.

When he did hold him, which was very seldom, it looked like he was holding a bowling ball that he was about ready to send down a bowling lane. Myron was becoming more comfortable with him but all that was lost because of what happened the morning of Chuck's baptism day. Although I thought it was funny, I really can't blame him.

We didn't have much counterspace in our kitchen so I used the kitchen table when I gave Chuck his bath, always waiting until after Myron had left for work. That morning, we were in a hurry and we had to share the table. Daddy could eat his breakfast at one end and Chuck and I were on the other end. I certainly did not anticipate what was about to happen. If I had known, I could have prevented it.

Anyone experienced in the care of baby boys knows what happens when cold air hits their bottoms. A geyser rivaling Old Faithful shot into the air and back down, as if on target, right into Daddy's cereal bowl. He wasn't amused. Nor was he amused later when we had to turn around and return home to get Chuck's baptismal shawl that I had forgotten to take along.

Chuck kept us on the move, too. When he was about six months old, we got the "No babies welcome," message once again. That time, we moved into a little white, unfurnished one-bedroom house even closer to downtown. We furnished it with odds and ends that we got from Myron's grandparents and from answering "For Sale" ads in the newspaper. By then, it was time for me to return to work.

I certainly didn't like having to leave Chuck but I was happy knowing that he would be in good hands. Aunt Eleanor, whose hearing had progressively become worse, was having a difficult time finding a job, so she was going to be his baby-sitter.

I don't know why but I didn't even consider returning to Great Northern Insurance Co. Instead, I applied at several other companies and all without success. My hearing had become worse, the interviews went badly and there wasn't a George Plaster to rescue me. There wasn't anything left to do but to go back to the factory.

I was hired at Lakeland Toy Factory and I worked on the assembly line there until it was destroyed by fire a few months later. I didn't go job hunting after that and for a good reason. We lost our baby-sitter in a very surprising way.

My youngest brother, Loyal, needed a baby-sitter. He, too, was losing his hearing and was having a difficult time. His wife was going back to her teaching job and they wanted Eleanor to live with them and take care of their children, Tim and Julie. She went.

One day, when Chuck and I were looking at the toys in a drugstore close to home, a display of beautiful dolls named Barbie, Ken and Midge caught my eye. They were just the kind of dolls that I would have loved to have had when I was a little girl. By pure whim, I bought a Barbie and a Ken and the patterns for making wardrobes for them. I went to Sears and bought some fabric and then went home and began to sew.

I had customers right away, Amy and Karen, two little neighbor girls. I kept right on sewing even after I had satisfied their demands and by October I had enough sewed up to place an ad in a local shopper.

I wasn't at all prepared for the response that I received. In no time, the clothes that I had sewed up were all gone and I was sewing night and day to keep up with the orders. By the end of the season, I had made enough money to purchase a brand new electric sewing machine. I was the proud owner of my very own business, Dora's Doll Clothes.

BAD NEWS

I didn't take any time off from sewing. I started again right after Christmas and I sold the clothes as fast as I could make them. Chuck took it all in stride but I made sure that he wasn't neglected.

The only thing he didn't like was when I was on the telephone taking orders and he made sure that I knew. Then he got into anything and everything. The day he opened the kitchen cabinet and pulled out a stack of mixing bowls that shattered all around, I knew I had a problem. I stopped taking orders and sold only what I had in stock.

My hearing definitely had gone down after Chuck was born but I was content with how my life was going. I don't think I would have gone looking for any more help if Myron hadn't had a severe attack of tonsillitis. Dr. George V. Tangen, Jr., the ENT specialist who had his office in the Medical Arts Building in Minneapolis, recommended that he have a tonsillectomy.

What should have been a routine surgery turned out to be much more than that. During the night, Myron began to hemorrhage. He wanted me to be there with him but I wasn't. I didn't hear the telephone ring. I feel as badly today as I did that morning when I walked into his hospital room and was told what had happened. The first time that my husband had needed me by his side, I failed him and I had my hearing loss to blame.

When Myron returned to Dr. Tangen for a checkup, I also had an appointment. Once again, I ended up sitting in a sound proof booth, trying with all my might to hear.

Dr. Tangen not only told us that I had a severe hearing loss, he counseled us. He was the one who first mentioned the Swartz sign or "red ear" and told me that it was an indication that my otoschlerosis was still progressing. He also told us some interesting facts about the disease.

He said that although it is hereditary, he thought that since Myron's hearing was normal, our children's hearing would likely not be affected. He told us that otosclerosis is more common in girls and it worsens during pregnancy. Quite likely, that is what had happened when I was pregnant with Chuck. More bone deposits had been laid down and my stapes bones had become refixed.

Leaving Dr. Tangen's office, I was quite a bit more knowledgeable about otoschlerosis and I also had a ray of hope. He would try a procedure called fenestration when the otoschlerosis had stabilized.

I was not patient. Now that I knew there was something out there that could help me, I didn't want to wait. I badgered Dr. Tangen unmercifully until he finally gave in. But had he waited two years or ten, the outcome would have been the same and I would not have been any better prepared.

I was wheeled into and out of the operating room of Abbott Hospital in record time. I can still see Dr. Tangen's smile of compassion and feel his disappointment when he came into my hospital room to tell me the bad news. When he entered my ear and saw that my oval window was almost completely obliterated by bone deposits, he chose not to continue rather than attempting to open it and risk deafness.

That was the first time that my hearing loss drove me to tears. I just could not handle the disappointment of that day and the realization that someday I would be deaf.

I didn't stay down for long, though, and everything Dr. Tangen, had told me about otosclerosis was ignored. I figured that since my hearing was already so bad and I couldn't be helped, I may as well have another baby. Had I been able to choose the baby's sex, I'm quite certain I would have acted in disregard there, too, and would have wanted a girl.

Warning Signs

Another baby meant moving again and this time into our very own two-bedroom home in New Brighton, Minn. It was the perfect neighborhood. There was an abundance of kids for Chuck to play with, little girls who needed clothes for their Barbie dolls and teen-age girls to baby-sit.

By then I had a seat right next to Myron in the Old Barn where I cheered for the Gopher Basketball Team. It was a much improved team for Coach Kundla and what we didn't realize then is that we were watching history in the making.

The first African-Americans, Lou Hudson, Archie Clark and Don Yates were on the team. And, wow, could they play. It was my first experience with the fast break and I have to admit that it frightened me. I expected them, at any time, to crash into one another or worse yet, to come sailing off the floor and into the spectators.

Once I got used to their style of play, I found it very enter- taining and had Lou Hudson landed in my lap, I wouldn't have minded at all. I had become quite enthralled by him. Not only did I admire his athleticism, I thought he had the best-looking pair of masculine legs I had ever seen.

Our new baby was expected to arrive right after Christmas but he waited until January 22. By then, he had outgrown his brother by 6 oz. and weighed in at 10 pounds, ¼ oz. I suppose he, too, wondered what I was talking about when I held him and told him he was a beautiful little baby. But he was—just as cute as his brother and also just as good.

We named him Kenneth LeRoy, after Kenneth, my friend in high school and my brother, LeRoy. Many years later, much to my surprise, I learned that my friend's middle name was also LeRoy. I would have expected the odds of that happening, with such a name as LeRoy, to be a million to one.

Kenny would have been a joy to take care of but along with him came a recurrence of wavy lines dancing around in my head. They came without warning and I knew the day that one occurred, while I was bathing Kenny, that I needed help.

I didn't get any beneficial help. All I received was a diagnosis of migraine headaches and the name, aura, that is given to the numbness, blind spots and wavy lines that precede an attack. I was told how lucky I was to experience the aura as then I could be helped with medicine that would ward off the migraine headaches.

It sounded great to me only there was something very wrong there. Never once had I experienced the migraine headache but I dutifully took the medicine. I don't know how long it took me to realize that it wasn't doing me any good. The auras still occurred. Finally, I stopped taking the medicine.

The auras occurred less frequently and were also much less severe. I also began to sense when one was about to occur so I felt much safer knowing that I was in control. The day I realized that I couldn't remember the last time I had experienced an episode was a very, very happy day for me.

I Didn't Want to Go

Kenny was a year old when Myron came home unexpectedly at noon one day and surprised me with the question, "How would you like to move to Iowa?" I was pretty excited! He had been

117

given a promotion into Data Processing but it entailed moving to Des Moines.

I was happy and proud of him and moving to another state sounded much more glamorous this time around because I would be with my family. But when we went down there for a visit, reality hit me and I cried myself to sleep in the motel room.

I didn't want to leave my friends who had grown to know and accept me. I was both frightened and weary of making new ones. But I kept my feelings locked up inside, packed our belongings and followed the moving van to the house we had rented in Des Moines.

Well, I didn't have to worry about getting acquainted with the neighbors. The neighborhood was composed of mostly elderly couples and the one neighbor who had boys Chuck could play with spent the summer at their cabin. That gave me ample time to sew Barbie fashions and I found out that the Iowa Barbies needed just as many fashions as they did in Minnesota.

By the time we bought our home in Ankeny, I was ready to come out of isolation and get on with the task of making new friends. It wasn't difficult. We were surrounded by young couples like us and the kids brought us together.

Chuck's first friend was a little boy named Johnny, who like me, was hearing impaired. When I met his mom, she immediately wanted me to pay a visit to Johnny's ENT specialist, Dr. Robert R. Updegraff, in Des Moines.

So it was that I found myself sitting in yet another sound-proof booth with the headphones strapped over my head.

After the audiological testing was completed, I had a consultation. I was told about a new procedure called a stapedectomy that was successfully being done for otosclerosis but like

Dr. Tangen, he did not want to attempt it. He referred me to Dr. C.M. Kos of the Otologic Medical Services in Iowa City, Iowa. I went to find him.

Back to the soundproof booth I went. This time it was much more difficult. Not only did I have to struggle to hear sounds, I now had to repeat words. In my mind, I can hear the "You will say the word ———," so clearly but what the words were that I was to say, I never knew.

At the end of the testing, Dr. Kos recommended that I have a stapedectomy on my left ear but I had to wait a long two months.

Finally, on August 10, 1967, I was wheeled into the operating room of Mercy Hospital in Iowa City, Iowa. All the while I wondered if I would be able to stay longer or if I would have to be pushed right out again.

I stayed and when Dr. Kos came to my hospital room after it was over, he brought me good news. Although he found that the otosclerosis had destroyed the oval window and that only the head of the stapes remained, he was able to perform the stapedectomy and the prognosis for improvement in my hearing was fair.

For the first time in ten years, I was able to hear without the help of a hearing aid. At night, when I lay reading in bed, I could hear the television from the living room. I no longer had to depend on Myron when Kenny woke up crying during the night. And, oh, how much easier and fun life was. It was pure delight to sit around the table and hear what was being said when the neighbors got together for morning coffee and to be able to joke back and forth with our friends in our bowling league was so satisfying.

I didn't think life could get any better but it did in a very surprising and unexpected way.

A KNOCK ON THE DOOR

One evening, when I was home alone with the boys, a knock came on the door. When I opened it, I saw a nice-looking, smiley Bible-toting young man standing on the porch. Other than when we had the boys baptized and attended church services a few times, we hadn't had much to do with religion.

So it is a surprise to me that I didn't shut the door with a not too polite, "I'm not interested." Instead, I invited him in and we spent the next hour visiting and entertaining Chuck and Kenny.

Pastor Donald Illian and Scott

He introduced himself as Pastor Donald Illian. He had been sent to Ankeny to get a Missouri Lutheran Mission Church built. When I heard him say, "Missouri Lutheran," our affiliation, I joined without a thought of first consulting with Myron.

When I told Myron, he didn't object and when the first organizational meeting rolled around, we were there sitting in the front row. From that day on, we were busy. Myron was elected secretary of the Council and I became involved with the youth.

My wish of becoming a teacher was somewhat fulfilled when I began to teach Sunday school. Then, in the summer, I taught a class at Vacation Bible School and when our Ladies' Guild was formed, I became vice-president.

Why, then, when I was able to live my life to the fullest, did I put it all in jeopardy and become pregnant again? The only reason I can give is that my arms felt empty and they wanted to hold a baby once again.

David Michael was born on June 29, 1969, his Grandma Tingelstad's birthday. He was a whopping 11 pounds and like his brothers, he, too, was born with red hair—so when I held him and told him he was a beautiful little baby, he must have thought I was out of my mind for how could an 11 pound baby with red hair be little and beautiful?

Although he was a big baby, he had health problems from the beginning. When he was only four months old, he was hospitalized with pneumonia. It was then that he and his daddy bonded.

Whenever Myron came to visit him, David became so animated that it was impossible for Myron not to respond. From that time on, they were fast friends. Myron took him along with him whenever he could. They went to softball and baseball games, on bike rides with David sitting behind, and as soon as he could sit alone, he went along to tractor pulls.

Myron had David with him so much that I was beginning to wonder who wanted another baby more, Myron or me. Then I discovered that I had something to think about that was far more worrisome.

My hearing had gone down so much that I had to resort to wearing hearing aids in both ears again. I also went back to Iowa City to find out if Dr. Kos would do a stapedectomy on my right ear. Since Eleanor was visiting us that summer, we made an appointment for her that same day to find out if she could be helped.

My fears were realized. My hearing had deteriorated in both ears and the Swartz (red ear) sign was pronounced in both ears also. Dr. Kos dissuaded me from having surgery at that time, prescribed sodium fluoride tablets to help slow down the process and told me to return in three months. Because there was so much nerve involvement, he was unable to help Eleanor.

It was much longer than three months before I returned. When David was eighteen months old, unexpectedly, Scott Matthew was on his way.

He was born October 9, 1971. When I held him and told him he was a beautiful little baby, he believed me. He was less than eight pounds and his head was covered with beautiful blonde hair.

Scott was a good baby but I was unable to take care of him. Just as they did after Kenny was born, my aura attacks returned, this time with such frequency that I couldn't be alone with him.

I was a regular visitor at the clinic but by the time I got to see the doctor, the episode would be over and I was normal in every way. Finally, though, he was convinced that I needed help and I was admitted to the hospital.

I spent a week undergoing tests. All the results were negative except that my blood sugar was a little high and I had a sinus infection. I was put on a diet and given medication for the sinus infection. The infections cleared up, I lost weight but the auras, although less frequent, continued.

I didn't waste any time in returning to see Dr. Kos. One week after my hospitalization, I was back in the sound proof booth. The hearing in my left ear had remained stable, the right had become worse. He told me to return in three months. If my left ear was the same, he would do the stapedectomy on my right ear.

On April 17, 1972, Dr. Kos performed the stapedectomy on my right ear and, again, he brought me good news when he came to my hospital room. The otosclerosis was even more pronounced than in my left ear but the prognosis for improvement in my hearing was good.

After that, I saw Dr. Kos only once when I returned to have the packing removed. In the six years we had lived in Iowa, I had beaten a path to his door. The part that he had in my journey, he had performed well and now it was out of his hands.

Six months later, as if it was all planned, we journeyed back to Minnesota.

Bruce Motor Freight was sold to Mid-American Trucking Lines in Kansas City, Mo. Myron could have been transferred there but he chose not to go. He began working for Briggs Transportation in the office of the Ankeny Terminal. The home office was in St. Paul.

Me and my four boys-Kenny, me and Scott, Chuck, David

One day, just as he had done six years previously, he came home unexpectedly at noon. Just like before, he had the same question for me, "How would you like to move—not to North Dakota, Wisconsin or California—but to Minnesota. I very emphatically answered, "Yes!" We were going home.

So much had happened in the six years we had been gone. I had my family of four and I got them without having to resort to deception or trickery. Myron had a better job and my hearing was so much better than when I left.

But most important of all was that our lives had been put in order. This time when we followed the moving van to our new home, God didn't have to tag along behind. We invited him to journey with us. After all, I didn't want to lose my travel agent, the best in the business.

PART SIX

JUST A MATTER OF TIME

But I didn't break down. Instead, my distress turned to anger. I left feeling so disillusioned with the University of Minnesota that I vowed never to return.

I made one more vow that day. I vowed that if I became deaf, rather than become a burden to my family, I would leave home.

Fortunately, we were not wealthy. Had we been, I may have been fool enough to go. What with the added expenses of my ear surgeries, the need to always buy hearing aids, their repair and batteries, Myron couldn't afford to support two households! Besides, how would I ever have been able to choose which two boys to take with me?

I am more and more convinced that our happiness or unhappiness depends far more on the way we meet the events of life, then on the nature of those events themselves.

Alexander Humboldt

Just as surely as I believe that God placed Mama and Papa in the right spot some twenty-five years previously, I believe that he placed Myron and me where he wanted us to be.

After having spent six years in the small town of Ankeny, Iowa, we were apprehensive about raising our four boys in the Twin Cities. When we began our search for a home and accidentally stumbled upon a newly built house in the little city of Spring Lake Park, just north of Minneapolis, it was like a breath of fresh air.

When we found Prince of Peace Lutheran Church, Missouri Synod, only a few blocks away with a sign advertising their Christian Day School, we knew that was where we wanted to live.

The location was perfect in yet another way. I had tried to learn how to drive while we lived in Iowa but I gave up when I found out that I couldn't have the roads all to myself and had to share them with others. After that, I relied on my bicycle or I walked to where I needed to go.

When we drove around the neighborhood and saw all the parks, the medical and dental clinics, the hospital, schools and the newly opened Northtown Mall all within a few blocks of the house, we went in search of a telephone so we could call the Realtor. We moved in a few days before Thanksgiving.

I wasn't nervous about meeting the neighbors as I had been when I left Minnesota; now I was overly eager to make new friends. Wintertime, when they were all snug in their homes, proved to be a bad time to move. Getting involved with church activities was the way to go. We transferred our membership from St. Paul's in Ankeny, enrolled Chuck and Kenny in the school and we got busy.

We came at the most opportune time on the church calendar. It was election time and there was a need to fill the ballot for church officers. Myron graciously agreed to having his name added as secretary. He was elected.

There also was a need for a Sunday school superintendent and when it became known that he had served in that capacity at St. Paul's, he got that job, too.

I began to teach the Sunday school class for three-year-olds. I was elected vice-president of LWML (Lutheran Women's Missionary League). I joined a ladies' circle and I got involved with the school.

The classes in the Ankeny schools had been large and the boys weren't doing too well so with the smaller classes and the devoted teachers at Prince of Peace, they thrived. An added incentive was a strong physical education program with traveling basketball and football teams and track meets in the spring.

Then, too, the city of Spring Lake Park had a strong parks and recreation program with in-house basketball for the youth and we became involved with that. Thus the foundation was laid for what would be our family's entertainment for the next eighteen years.

Even though I had been kept busy all winter, by spring I was anxious to meet the neighbors. But I certainly wasn't expecting the manner in which it occurred.

Seems the neighbors were afraid of the family with four boys and the "new kids in town" weren't exactly welcomed. Instead, they were accused of every petty crime that happened in the neighborhood.

That's how I met my neighbors and after the first few confrontations, I was ready to turn my hearing aids off or to pack up and move back to Iowa. But I stood my ground. Where I got the stamina, I don't know as I am by nature very sensitive. By the time I had hung up the telephone or said a "good-bye" at the door, we were friends.

When the guilty culprits were caught and brought to justice, we received an apology. In the twenty-five years since that we have lived as neighbors, we have lived harmoniously side by side without any problems of any great proportion.

The boys did outnumber the girls, another family with four was our back door neighbor, so there were always the sounds of a baseball game in the air but few girls playing with Barbie dolls. I had to look elsewhere for a clientele for my doll clothes.

I sewed all summer and into fall. By the end of October, I had boxes and boxes full of clothes ready to sell. I posted signs on telephone poles and I placed an ad in the local shopper. The telephone didn't ring and no one was beating a path to my door.

When I began to do my Christmas shopping, I found out why. Every nook and cranny of the corridors at the malls were filled with crafters sitting by their displays and selling their wares. Among them were several tables laden down with Barbie doll clothes.

I joined them at the spring sales and I have been a part of the crafters' world since. I didn't have to worry about whether or not my clothes would sell after that. Then I had to worry about having enough to sell as I kept my resolution not to take orders.

By the end of the first year, I was making a significant contribution to our family's finances and I was having fun doing so. I have not met a crafter I didn't like. Each is uniquely talented, hard working and most care about and lend their support to others.

I became steadfast friends with so many. Even competitors such as Marge, Marlys and Kathy became my friends. Some like Kathy and Gil and Nancy became like family and we requested placement next to each other.

Now, I know that during those first years when I was still able to hear, more groundwork was being laid for that time during my journey when I would need all the help and support I could get.

I DON'T WANT TO BE A BURDEN

It wasn't long after moving back to Minnesota that I began to wear binaural hearing aids once again. It was always my practice to put the left one in my ear first. Then I would test it with the "La-la-la" of my own voice. Then I would put the aid in my right ear.

One morning, for no particular reason, I put the aid in my right ear first. When I said my "La-la-la's," I couldn't hear them. I wasn't alarmed; I just thought the battery was dead. But when I put in a fresh one and I still couldn't hear, I thought *Oh, oh.*

I think you can imagine just how beautiful the "La-la-la" of my voice was when I put in my left aid. I hadn't noticed that my hearing had become worse and until that morning, I had been getting along okay.

I am amazed at the workings of the human mind or, at least, my own for unless I lost the hearing in that ear overnight, I had in my own mind, been able to hear with it. As soon as I realized that it was deaf, I began to have real problems. It was time, once again, to seek out the help of an ENT specialist.

On August 22, 1978, I returned to the University of Minnesota Otolaryngology Clinic. Even now, 20 years later, I have a difficult time speaking about that day.

I didn't find Dr. Boies, Sr. for he had retired several years before. Neither did I find the pleasant conditions that I remembered. The Lions International 5M had not yet arrived on the scene and the clinic was in total disarray.

There was a makeshift waiting room with folding chairs set up along the walls of a hallway. The Otolaryngology and Ophthalmology Departments were housed under one clinic. While I sat there waiting to be called into the examining room, my eyes took over the work of my ears. What I saw was very depressing.

There was a total lack of privacy. An elderly woman, wearing a patch over one eye, was helped to a chair near where Myron and I were seated. The patch was removed and in full view of all the other patients, she underwent an eye examination.

My heart went out to her as she struggled to read the eye chart. Her will to see was as strong as my will to hear and although she read every letter incorrectly, in her own mind she was able to see them.

The one positive thing about that visit was that I did have a thorough audiologic evaluation even though I didn't learn the results until I began to write *Journey Out of Silence*. Then, while reading my many hospital records, I became aware of just how significant they were. On August 22, 1997, exactly 19 years to the day, my understanding of spoken words had improved by as much as 100 percent.

I had a very brief examination by a doctor, just as long as it took to shake my hand and to hear him say, in a high pitched voice, "You don't hear well, do you?" I was taken aback by his remark. Certainly I knew that. That was why I was there, to find out why and to ask for his help. Thinking that I would have a consultation with him, I didn't respond.

But I didn't get that consultation. I was brought back to the row of chairs where I waited until I was taken to sit by a table and listen to two audiologists counsel me about hearing aids.

My first question was, "Am I going to talk to the doctor?"

They looked at each other and after some hesitation, answered, "No." My next question, "Isn't there anything that can be done to help me?" should have been directed to the doctor and I know that I put the audiologists on the spot. After even a longer hesitation, I received the same answer.

My mind was in such a turmoil by then that, however helpful the advice I received may have been, I was not receptive to it. Even if I was able to hear what they were telling me, I was not listening. All I wanted to do was to get away from there before I broke down.

But I didn't break down. Instead, my distress turned to anger. I left feeling so disillusioned with the University of Minnesota that I vowed never to return. I made one more vow that day. I vowed that if I became deaf, rather than become a burden to my family, I would leave home.

Fortunately, we were not wealthy. Had we been, I may have been fool enough to go. What with the added expenses of my ear surgeries, the need to always buy hearing aids, their repair and batteries, Myron couldn't afford to support two households! Besides, how would I ever have been able to choose which two boys to take with me?

I CAN, TOO, STILL HEAR

When I thought about this time of my journey, it struck me just how similar those years were to my high school years. Even the manner in which I lost my hearing was the same. It didn't occur suddenly; it happened very gradually over the next ten years.

I found myself resorting more and more to using the same tactics that helped me survive my teen years. I had to be more alert again and once again, strangers threatened me. But I found out that this time around, it wasn't as easy to avoid them. At the time, I felt that they were there just to torture me but now I think of them as angels who were sent to keep me in the world.

They appeared everywhere—in the malls, on my walks, and I wasn't even safe sitting in the privacy of my own front yard. One after another, a car would stop, some even swerving over from an opposite lane just to get closer to me. I was asked the directions to get from one end of Spring Lake Park to the other and sometimes even beyond.

Most of the time I couldn't hear where the occupants of the cars wanted to go and I would have to tell them I didn't know but the times that I did were a major accomplishment. Sometimes, too, there was humor.

Early one morning as I was walking to the mall, a service van stopped. The driver leaned over and asked, "Can you tell me where West-B is?"

I understood that clearly but I had no idea whatsoever where it could be. He had a clipboard in his hand and I glanced at the crude map that he had drawn. According to his map, he should have been only a couple of blocks away. And he was but it wasn't West-B like he had been told. It was Westby, a little street only a few blocks from where we lived. We both got a big laugh out of that. He was able to keep his appointment and for a while, I was floating on air.

My neighbors never gave up on me, either, even though it must have been exasperating listening to me chatter away. Long after I became deaf, they went that extra mile to keep me a part of the neighborhood. Even after I lost the ability to use the telephone, they didn't quit. They called in the evening when Myron was home with invitations for morning coffee, to Tupperware and other parties, or to go out to lunch.

Steadfast friends—1978
JoAnn, Barb, Pat, Colleen

I was still able to hear the amplified ring of the telephone so I was aware of when someone was calling but I avoided answering it if I could. Our neighbors, friends and most relatives knew that I couldn't hear well, even with the amplifier, so most of the calls were for Chuck, Ken or David.

Scott was still too little to get calls, but after I gave him a lesson on the etiquette of answering, he became my helpmate. It was only recently that I learned just how well he handled that responsibility.

If the caller asked, "Is Chuck there?" or "Is Ken there?" or "Is Dave there?", he was very truthful and right to the point. If they were home, he answered "Yes," and, if not, he said, "No." Then he hung up. Consequently, many a message went unreturned.

Living away from my relatives made it easy for me to keep them in the dark about just how bad my hearing was becoming. But the day came when it was inevitable and, oddly enough, it was the telephone that did the revealing.

My brother, Herbert, called long distance and other than refusing to talk to him, I had no other choice than to put the phone to my ear. I couldn't detect much more than his voice and after only a short time, I gave up and handed the telephone to Kenny.

The news was out of the bag and it spread like wildfire among my relatives. Of course, I didn't like that. I had alot of hearing left. It was only when I was on the telephone that I couldn't hear.

STOP THE WORLD AND LET ME OFF

You will succeed best when you put the restless, anxious side of affairs out of mind, and allow the restful side to live in your thoughts.

Margaret Stowe

Oh, how much better life would have been for both Myron and me if I had done that instead of becoming the troubled, fretful person that I became.

I had to give up teaching Sunday school and my attendance at Ladies' Guild and Circle meetings became less and less frequent until I quit attending altogether. I did continue to socialize with the neighbors. But it was so tiring and frustrating that by the time Myron got home from work, I was zapped and I took it out on him.

I was so testy and unreasonable that any little thing set me off. Myron and I had lost our ability to communicate so I had to guess at what he said and my guesses were not at all good ones. I didn't like myself and I didn't want him to like me, either. I would go into the bedroom, slam the door behind me and lay on our bed and cry.

Myron very seldom came in to console me. After all, he hadn't said or done anything to hurt me. It was pure imagination on my part with a dash of self pity and a big side dish of egotism. Here I was almost deaf and I was doing everything that a person with normal hearing could do. *Certainly,* I thought, *I was deserving of praise, not criticism.* I took out my frustrations on my sewing machine. My mind kept pace, fast and furious with my sewing.

A deaf person spends a lot of time in thought and while I sewed, my thoughts ran rampant. What I was thinking was unfit for my deaf ears. I worked very hard at making myself miserable—always with the idea that I would be so much better living alone and plotting ways to do so.

Something would always happen to get me back to thinking rationally and everything would run smoothly for a while. Then something would happen to set me off again. It was a vicious circle. I spent way too many precious hours making life miserable for myself and far more so for Myron. Thankfully, none of our boys was aware of what was going on behind the scenes.

I often wondered about that but I was afraid of what I would hear if I asked. One evening when our oldest son, Chuck, stopped in, I had the perfect opportunity. What he told me filled my heart with pride for him and it also released me of any feelings of guilt.

I asked him, "What was it like growing up with a mom who couldn't hear? Did you feel threatened by it and did I embarrass you?"

He looked at me as though I didn't know what I was talking about and said, "Mom, I was always able to talk to you. It was never an issue because you never made it one."

A few days later, I asked our youngest son, Scott, the same questions. He thought I was joking.

I have yet to ask Kenny and David but I am confident that they would answer in much the same way and I am very thankful for that. What I received from them by far outweighs what I gave them and they smoothed many a bump along my journey.

THEY GAVE TO ME

All four of our sons were athletic. From the winter of 1972, when Chuck began to play basketball at Prince of Peace School and in the city league, Myron and I were kept busy.

The City of Spring Lake Park has an excellent parks and recreation program for the youth and our family used it over and over. Not only did it benefit the boys, it provided Myron and me with years of the best entertainment possible. Myron was also given the opportunity to use his love and knowledge of the games.

Back row—left to right: Chuck, Dave, Myron, Scott, me, Kenny.

He spent many hours coaching. In winter, he coached a basketball team and his summers were filled with baseball and softball, sometimes coaching both. All the while, I was on the sidelines enthusiastically cheering them on.

They graduated, one by one, from the city teams to Jr. High and High School sports. There was football in the fall, basketball in winter and baseball in spring with a smattering of softball thrown in during the summer.

Ken, Scott, Dave, Chuck

We didn't miss many games. We sat through football games in 0° weather, huddled together in blankets, or under umbrellas and wrapped in plastic during downpours of rain. In the summer, we sat under the heat of the scorching sun watching baseball and softball games.

It was a great deal more comfortable at the basketball games. I had the best vantage point at the very top of the bleachers but I wasn't there for the visual advantages it provided. It somewhat secluded me from the other spectators, freeing me from having to speak to them.

No, I wasn't anti-social; I just wasn't able to hear and I'm sure the parents who didn't know me thought I was stand-off-ish or, heaven forbid, shy. I wasn't either and it hurt terribly not to be able to share the camaraderie that they had with one another.

Scott, Dave, Kenny, Chuck and Myron

The world didn't stop. It picked up speed, faster and faster it went. The boys were growing up and girls entered the picture. The boys had always come and gone with their friends and as long as they were boys, I was comfortable. But when they began bringing girls home for Mom and Dad to meet, I felt threatened. Not out of jealousy or possessiveness but fear. I felt compelled to chat with them but I knew that it would be very difficult.

I didn't need to worry. I am so deeply thankful and proud of the way the boys handled that part of their lives too. They had so thoroughly "schooled" the girls about my disability that there wasn't a thread of discomfort or embarrassment when they were introduced.

Brandon

We got along well. So well, in fact, that I was hurt right along with the girls when there was a "break-up." There were a few times, probably from remembrances of my own experiences in high school, when I meddled and tried to get them back together. If my meddling didn't succeed, they would come over and cry on my shoulder.

But not so with Allison, who later became David's wife. She used a different tactic, one that proved just how wise she is. When David got the idea that he wanted to be free, she let him go.

For a time, circumstances in Allison's family made it necessary for her to live with us and during that time, she became very dear to me. So when the break-up came, I felt I had lost a daughter. By then I had learned not to meddle in the boys' love lives and I let her go.

She wrote me several letters. In one she wrote, "If you love someone, set him free—if he comes back, it was meant to be."

This is just what happened. They have been married for almost three years. On January 2, 1998, Myron's birthday, they presented us with a beautiful little grandson, Brandon David.

THAT'S OKAY——THAT'S ALL RIGHT

By 1984, the Tingelstad family had grown to number 25 grandchildren and step-grandchildren. Only one niece, LeRoy's daughter Diane, was experiencing hearing problems and those were unrelated to otoschlerosis. All the grandchildren, except for my sons David and Scott, should have safely passed the age when symptoms would begin to show.

I found out just how wrong I was while visiting my brother Loyal's family. Their lovely daughter, Julie, who had just graduated from Concordia College, Moorhead, Minn. had been diagnosed as having otosclerosis and was scheduled to have a stapedectomy at the Mayo Clinic in Rochester, Minn.

I was heartbroken. She wanted to be an English teacher and all I could think about was that I didn't want her to have to give up her dream like I had to. I told her, from my heart, "Julie, I don't have much hearing left but if I could give it to you, I would gladly do so."

Not long after, she had a successful stapedectomy and she began teaching Senior High English in Long Prairie, Minn. A short time later, she underwent a second one that also was successful. She met and married Dave, took a few years off to raise Jenna and Jacob and is now back at teaching.

During the same time, my brother, Loyal, also underwent two consecutive stapedectomies at the Mayo Clinic. One was successful and one was not. He continues to be helped with the use of a hearing aid.

141

I figured that I had used up all my options for recovering my hearing by surgery but I had not yet given up on hearing aids. In all the years I had visited hearing aid dealerships, not one had referred me to an ear specialist. Now, when I was told to visit one, it only succeeded in putting my mind in turmoil. Even more surprising was that I was referred to the same specialist Julie and my brother had at the Mayo Clinic, Dr. Thomas J. McDonald.

I wasn't very optimistic. After undergoing four surgeries, I didn't think there was anything more that could be done for me. That was the second time I was brought to tears. I had gone seeking a stronger hearing aid and now, instead, I was going to try to regain my hearing. When we drove into our driveway, I gave it all up and let the tears flow.

Our son, David, turned around from the front seat where he was sitting, smiled at me and said, "That's Okay—That's all right. Come on, Mom, Fight! Fight! Fight!" With that rallying cry ringing in my ears, Myron and I journeyed to Rochester.

The waiting room was very large and there were more patients than I had ever seen in one room. But even in all that hustle and bustle, I didn't lose my identity and I was treated with respect and compassion. I felt right at home in the sound proof room, too, as the audiologic evaluation was much the same as it had been in Iowa City.

There was a lengthy wait before I saw Dr. McDonald but when he did come into the examining room, he gave me all the time I needed. We discussed the advantages and disadvantages of undergoing yet another stapedectomy. We agreed that since I had once shown an improvement in the hearing of my right ear, although it was brief, we would try one more time.

No, Doctor, You Must Be Mistaken

By then, my optimism had returned and I confidently began to tell everyone that I was going to regain my hearing. I also talked to God about it. Not in prayer or "Thy will be done," instead, I bargained with him. I told him if my hearing was restored, I would teach Sunday school again, I'd serve as president of the Ladies' Guild; I would do anything he wanted me to do.

I found out that either God had gone deaf on me, that he knew I would not keep my part of the bargain, that he had other plans for me or that you can't strike bargains with him.

On June 2, 1985, Myron, Scott and I walked into the Mayo Clinic and spent the day riding the elevator going from floor to floor for preoperative tests. I was admitted to Methodist Hospital that evening with my surgery scheduled for early morning.

It was noon before I was wheeled into the operating room. While I waited, Dr. Miettunen, Dr. McDonald's resident, visited me. When he read my chart and saw that I was scheduled for yet another stapedectomy, he was confused.

He asked, "Are you going to have a cochlear implant?"

I didn't know what that was but I certainly was not going to have it and I told him so.

That was a close call and what saved me was the usable hearing that still remained in my left ear. Had I undergone the implant then, quite likely I would be hearing only sounds and the rhythm of voices instead of the resonance that I am now enjoying.

In the 14 years since I had my last stapedectomy, there had been changes in the procedure so I was in the operating room for a longer period of time. I didn't hear any scratching, scraping or the whir of a drill and I didn't hear Dr. McDonald when he spoke to me so I sensed that things were not going well.

I remember, too, that my anesthesiologist held my hand the entire time. As the surgery progressed, so did the pressure of her hand. That, too, somehow conveyed that message to me. Yet, when I was back in my room, I could hear so much better. The voices of the nurses were clear and I could hear the television so well.

When Dr. McDonald came into my room and told me that I didn't have any improvement, I said, "No, Doctor, you're mistaken," and I argued with him.

If the hearing in my right ear hadn't improved, I thought, *then my left ear must be better.*

I asked him if some how that had happened. I also asked him if our ears worked independently of each other.

He answered, "We don't know that."

I went right back to riding the waves of Euphoria. On the drive home, I could hear the cars as they whizzed by and the roar of the semis was deafening.

That evening when Myron mowed the yard, I was able to hear the lawn mower as he passed under the window of our bedroom. As I watched the Twins game, I could hear the baseball as it hit the leather of the catcher's mitt and the whack of the bat as it sent the ball sailing into the stands.

Then one morning, not long after, I woke up with my tinnitus roaring like a lion and hissing like a boa constrictor. It was persistent and nothing short of sleep would relieve it. I went to sleep hearing it and I woke up hearing it.

One day, out of sheer desperation, I went for a walk. That was the therapy I needed. I had found a way to, not shut it off, but put it out of my mind. That was the start of my daily walks.

When I returned to the Mayo Clinic, I took Dr. McDonald at his word. I had not regained any hearing. He prescribed

Tranxene in hopes of lessening the tinnitus and as a precautionary measure, I had a CT scan.

He told me, "No more ear surgeries."

I don't know if that included a cochlear implant or not. The results of the CT scan came back negative but the tinnitus and the auras, although less frequent and severe, continued.

I purchased my last hearing aid a few months later and I wore it only a short time before I realized it was not helping me. I placed it in a little jewelry box that my sister had given me. It remained there for ten years. Then I placed it, once again, in my ear—not in hopes that it would help me hear but rather to prove that it couldn't.

YESTERDAY'S TOMORROW

I'm sitting on the edge of tomorrow
watching the sun go down today.
I do not know if there'll be joy or sorrow
or will my life be put in disarray?

I'm sitting on the edge of tomorrow
watching the stars come out to play.
Will there be smiles or will I need to borrow
somebody's shoulder on which to cry?

I'm sitting on the edge of tomorrow
When I go to bed tonight, I'll pray.
I'll ask that God will make me strong so
I can meet whatever comes my way.

I'm sitting on the dawn of yesterday's tomorrow
watching the sun rise in the sky.
I know since God takes care of all the sparrows
I'll trust that he'll not pass me by.

I'm sitting on the edge of yesterday's tomorrow
I'm feeling not a bit afraid.
I know that I need not have worried 'bout tomorrow
'cause yesterday's tomorrow was today.

Spring 1993

PART SEVEN

BLOWING IN THE WIND

I will never say that I was okay with being deaf but, somehow, after all the time that I had spent wondering when it would happen, it was a relief when it did. I no longer had to struggle to hear as the biggest and best of all struggles couldn't help me. Then, too, though I don't think of it as giving up hope, after having undergone five surgeries I no longer thought there would be any more and I began to adjust to being deaf for the rest of my life.

In spite of illness, in spite even of the archenemy sorrow, one can remain alive long past the usual date of disintegration if one is unafraid of change, insatiable in intellectual curiosity, interested in big things, and happy in small ways.

Edith Wharton

I keep going, going, going
Down the highway of life.
I keep going, going, going
Down the highway of life.
'Cause my Mama keeps telling me
There's someone watching over me
My God.

I woke up one morning with that song, that I had never heard, playing over and over in my head. Until someone tells me otherwise, I will always think of it as a message from Mama telling me never to give up.

Not long before, she had unexpectedly passed away and it had been a very traumatic time for her family and friends. The church was packed for her funeral. It seemed as though the entire town of Pelican Rapids, Minn. had come to say their "Good-byes" and to comfort her family.

During lunch in the basement of Trinity Lutheran Church, old friends and relatives I hadn't seen for years came to me with condolences. Very few knew that I was deaf so it was an extremely difficult time for me. Not only was I unable to understand what they said, I did not know who they were.

I had a pad and pen along with me. I pulled it out of my purse and resorted to having them write notes to me. That was the start of a brand new way for others to communicate with me.

It was also a turning point of my journey. I finally came to realize that however much I didn't want to be deaf, God had given me a good life and from now on, it was up to me what I would do with it.

I still spent a great deal of time in thought as I sat sewing but now I made a conscious effort to think good thoughts. I no longer thought about the things that I could no longer do and concentrated on what I could do. And, in the process, I discovered that there were many.

Oh, I still had my "down times" but when I found myself getting gloomy, I took to the streets. Sometimes two or three times a day. One morning, I stopped in at the McDonald's Restaurant that was a few blocks from home. The friendly atmosphere and just being there with others as they came and went calmed me. I began stopping more and more often until I became a regular morning coffee visitor.

McDonald's Angels

Placing an order at a fast food restaurant never was one of my favorite things. In fact, it was a pain with all the questions that had to be answered. I never could understand why, when I ordered a hamburger, I was asked, "Do you want cheese on it?" or if I ordered a sausage McMuffin, I was asked, "Do you want it with egg?"

No matter how concise I was, there was always something that I forgot. Like failing to tell them that I would be eating "in" or that I wanted regular coffee or what size fries I wanted.

So discovering what my grandson, Jeffery, now calls "Grandma's McDonald's," where no unnecessary questions were asked, was like a breath of fresh air. Oh, there were times when a new girl began cashiering that were a bit hard but as soon as Machelle or Sandy caught my predicament, they were informed. Thus, it made for a pleasant break in my day, one in which I was free from all stress and frustration.

I even began to lose my fear of strangers and I found out that they were just friends I had not met. Most were men. I did not intentionally try to meet men, mind you, but very few women are out that early in the morning.

My first acquaintances were Al and Bill and it was Al who approached me first. I didn't like to just sit and while away the time that I spent there so I brought paper and pen with me and I wrote letters. Maybe that was what caught his eye and he thought I needed a break from all that writing.

One morning when I was busy writing, he walked by and sheepishly laid a typewritten article on my table. I thought I'd better read it and I'm certainly glad I did. It was so funny that I couldn't keep from laughing out loud. I have kept it and I want to share it with you.

Subject: a day brightener
Check the facilities before making the trip!

This story concerns a nice little old lady who was a bit old- fashioned. She was planning a week's vacation in Kansas at a particular ranch and she wanted to make sure of the accommodations first. Uppermost in her mind was the toilet facilities but she couldn't bring herself to write "toilet" in a letter.

After considerable deliberation, she settled on "bathroom commode," but when she rewrote the letter to the ranch, she referred to the bathroom commode as the "B.C."

"Does the ranch have its own B.C.?" is what she actually wrote. The ranch owner was baffled by the euphemism so he showed the letter around to several neighbors but they couldn't decipher it, either.

Finally, the ranch owner figured she must be referring to the location of the local Baptist Church so he sat himself down and wrote, "Dear Madam, I regret very much the delay in answering your letter but I now take the pleasure of informing you that a B.C. is locat-

ed nine miles north of the ranch and is capable of seating 250 people at one time.

"I must admit it is quite a distance away if you are in the habit of going regularly but, no doubt, you will be pleased to know that a great number of people take their lunches along and make a day of it. They usually arrive early and stay late.

"The last time my wife and I went was six years ago and it was so crowded we had to stand up the whole time we were there. It may interest you to know there is a supper planned to raise money to buy more seats. They're going to hold it in the basement of the B.C.

"I would like to say it pains me very much not to be able to go more regularly but it was surely no lack of desire on my part; as we grow older, it seems to be more of an effort, particularly in cold weather.

"If you do decide to come to our ranch, perhaps I could go with you the first time, sit with you and introduce you to all the folks. Remember, this is a friendly community."

It certainly was a day brightener and it proved to be a perfect party mixer and the start of a wonderful friendship.

After that, Al began bringing me other little stories, many that came from his hometown, Bagley, Minn., newspaper. All were amusing and interesting but none were quite as funny as that first one he brought me.

Then Bill, Al's friend, got into the act and I was left with little time in which to write my letters. Instead, the three of us began to write what I truly think of as "love notes" to one another. Of anything I have thrown away over the years, those notes are among the things I wish I had saved.

We talked about everything under the sun. Al had recently retired after 23 years with the Minnesota Highway Department. He didn't tell me stories about those years, though. He proudly spoke of his family, especially his little grandson, and of his day to day activities.

Bill, the more intellectual of the two, kept me informed on the workings of the federal government and he took me back to World War II when he was an aviation radioman flying in the bombers tracking enemy submarines and supply ships. He also told me stories of when, after the war, he was one of the first five employees of Medtronics, working out of a garage of a private home in N.E. Minneapolis.

We certainly had our share of laughs, too. They both like to tease and once my guard went down, I gave it right back to them. The better acquainted we became, the more open I was in discussing my hearing loss.

Every so often one would ask me when I was going to go back to a doctor. My answer was always the same, "There isn't any more that can be done for me."

GOD ISN'T FINISHED WITH ME YET

When one door of happiness closes, another opens, but often we look so long at the closed door that we do not see the one which has opened for us."

Helen Keller

I will never say that I was okay with being deaf but, somehow, after all the time that I had spent wondering when it would happen, it was a relief when it did. I no longer had to struggle to hear as the biggest and best of all struggles couldn't help me. Then, too, though I don't think of it as giving up hope, after having undergone five surgeries I no longer

153

thought there would be any more and I began to adjust to being deaf for the rest of my life.

I had used an amplified telephone for many years and my sister had a flashing alarm clock to wake us when we lived together but I had not thought of getting any other devices. I sent off for a catalog. When it arrived, I looked at it like a child looking at a Christmas Toy catalog.

Not being able to hear the doorbell was especially irksome. If I was expecting a service man, I either had to spend the entire one to four hours sitting by the window watching for him or wearing a path in the carpet going back and forth from one room to another. A doorbell with a light that came on when it was pressed was number one on my list.

We never did get around to ordering one but I did get something else. In the fall of 1987 in the Education Building of the Minnesota State Fair, I was introduced to closed-captioned TV.

Just in time for the Minnesota Twins-Cleveland Indians World Series, Myron surprised me by bringing one home for me. My world of silence came to life. How great it was to be able to "hear" what the announcers were saying about the individual players, to "hear" "The Star-Spangled Banner" being sung, the deafening roar of the crowd and the play-by-play commentator.

I got so wrapped up reading the play-by-play that I wasn't watching the action and I missed many of the exciting plays, such as Kirby Puckett's leaping catches and Kent Hrbek's controversial play at first base.

After a couple of nights of that, I only "listened" to what the announcers had to say before the game and the singing of "The Star-Spangled Banner." Then I turned the closed-captioning off and enjoyed watching the action. As soon as the game was over,

I turned the captioning on so as not to miss a single word of the excitement and praise.

That continued to be my habit when I watched most sports events but not so with other programs. To be able to laugh along with Myron was pretty wonderful. And, when one after another, local news channels began captioning their evening news broadcasts, I was kept up on the happenings of the world around me.

(The one thing that upsets me is that the weather report is not captioned and that a way has not yet been implemented to more fully include the deaf during severe storm warnings.)

When I wasn't enjoying the wonders of closed captioning, I was reading. I always liked to read but over the years, other than reading umpteen books to the boys, I had grown away from reading for my own enjoyment.

When my crafter friend, Nancy, introduced me to the writings of Danielle Steele, that changed. I read all her books, some twice. Then I discovered LaVeryle Spencer's writings, many of which portrayed life in Minnesota, something that was of deep interest to me.

I began to write my own love stories. Not fiction but true life stories of growing up surrounded by the love of Mama, Papa, my brothers and sister. My first attempt was small. It included the years 1938-1945 when we lived in the country. The title is *Golden Memories*. Intentionally, I wrote it in the way that I remembered events. I wanted it to evoke the memories of my family and it did.

It didn't take long before I was hearing, "That's not how it happened—it happened like this," or "I didn't do that, he did." Secretly, though, I think I gave an accurate account of those years. It is their memories that had become rusty over the years.

When that was finished, I began to dabble in poetry. Once again, I wrote only about life while I was growing up. The title of that is "Golden Memories - In Verse." I figured that was the extent of my writing but I was wrong. Two years later, I received a very unusual request from my sister.

One night, in a dream, she had a vision of a time when she and our brothers Alvin, Herbert and Loyal came home from school on a cold, winter's day. She remembered that when I was in school, I liked to draw and she requested that I capture the scene on paper.

I bought a sketch pad and went to work. My hand flew across the paper and by the end of the day, when Myron came home from work, the finished product was laying on the kitchen table. Not only had I fulfilled her wish, I had portrayed the entire family.

Papa was out with his horses Doc and Florry, Milan was trudging through the snow, his arms laden down with an armful of wood. Mama was outside the door feeding our cat while LeRoy was bringing in a pail of water. I was playing in the snow. A long plumage of smoke drifted from the chimney of our little white house, inviting them into its warmth. They were

Coming Home

The road was long
The hill was steep
It was so cold
and the snow was deep.

The wind through their coats
Began to creep
They wanted to rest
Their weary feet.

But on they trudged
And it wasn't long
'till they saw the smoke
They were "coming home."

Another door was flung wide open for me. I did an entire biography in sketches that I titled *Garden of Memories*. That was capped off in March 1989 when I combined my sketching with limericks to tell the story of "The Fabulous Seven and Two."

In 1991, I took on a much larger task. Once again, I wrote my autobiography. This time I included my life up until I graduated in 1956. I did not mention my hearing impairment.

Somewhere, in each of my writings, I have written the words, "God isn't finished with me yet."

I JUST LOOK THAT WAY

I didn't quit sewing and participating in craft sales. In fact, with fewer distractions I was able to sew more. But I know, without the patience, help and love that Nancy, Gil and Kathy gave me, I would never have had the stamina to continue. Just knowing that they were right there by my side helped put me at ease.

The only stressful time was when I was setting up my display. Then, just as it happened when I was on my walks, I was bombarded with "angels" asking me directions. One after another they came.

"Where's the ladies' room?"

"What time is it?"

"How long are you here?"

"What time do you close?"

It happened so frequently that my friends began calling me the "Information Booth."

The reason for that happening was quite obvious. Once again, I had to be alert, my eyes doing the work of my ears. My eyes were rarely downcast so I was the most logical person to approach.

One morning when my brother, Herbert, was helping me set up, I mentioned this to him. Just then a lady breezed up to me, smiled and asked me a question. Of course, I wasn't able to hear her so my brother answered her. When she left, he began to laugh and told me what she had said. It confirmed my suspicions.

She had said, "You look like someone who knows everything."

Nice compliment but, no, I didn't know everything. I just looked that way.

I would dearly have liked to have heard the comments of the shoppers, even the negative ones. Unless I sensed that a customer needed help, I never initiated a conversation. Then, if I was unable to understand after the second try at lip-reading, I took out my pad and paper and asked them to write what they wanted.

It wasn't often that they didn't accommodate me but when they didn't, I rationalized that I was the one who was losing a sale and I wasn't harming anyone else. But, actually, I believe that although it was never my intention, when they realized I was deaf, many bought more than they had planned out of the goodness of their hearts.

It was during one unusually slow day, after I sensed I had made two such sales, that I confided my suspicions to one of my fellow crafters.

"Aha!" she said, "I'm going to pretend that I'm blind!"

Sometimes, though, asking my customers to write notes to me didn't always work. Sometimes it was downright embarrassing, not to me but to the shopper.

One day, a young girl stopped by my table, not to purchase doll clothes but to find out how to get somewhere. I tried as hard as I could to understand her but I just could not figure out where it was she wanted to go. Finally, I handed her my ever-present pad and pen and told her to write where she wanted to go.

She didn't hesitate for a second but when she handed the pad back to me, I was as confused as ever. Her spelling was so bad that I could not read what she had written. I was about at my wit's end but she wasn't. She plodded right along. Finally, I got it! She wanted to know how to get to the nearby Holiday Inn.

After all that time, I wasn't even able to help her. I didn't know where it was. I'm sure that when she finally got there, she was tired out from all that haggling with me and jumped right into bed.

By the time I got home that night, I certainly was tired as I had done more haggling. Whenever I speak at a Lions' International 5M function, I tell one of my favorite stories. It never fails to draw a laugh and it also shows just what a deaf person is up against when ordering in a restaurant, particularly a fast food restaurant.

That same evening, Myron had a previous engagement and was unable to pick me up so Chuck, our oldest son, was going to come but he would be late. I told him I would walk over to the nearby fast food restaurant and wait for him there.

I was tired after a long, hard day and I wasn't in any mood to go through the hassles of ordering anything more than a cup of coffee. Besides, it was the supper hour and I had no intention of holding up the long line of people. Confidently, I walked up to the counter and this is the quiz I had to take. I began to wonder if I would ever get that cup of coffee.

"May I help you?"

"I'd like a cup of coffee, please."

"Do you want it to go?"

"No, I'll drink it here." (I wondered, *Is the coffee to go different?*)

"Do you want small or large?"

"Small."

"Regular or decaf?"

"Regular."

"Do you want cream?"

"No."

"Do you want sugar?"

"No."

Whew! She was done with the questioning and I had known all the answers.

I handed her the $5 bill that I had stuck in my pocket. That drew one more question, "Do you have anything smaller?"

"No, I don't." I got that question right, too!

I should have quit while I was ahead but I was feeling so proud of myself that when I saw the display of cookies by the cash register, I thought I would order one of those, too. I noticed there were two different kinds. I ordered chocolate chip.

She took it out but before she would give it to me, I had to answer one more question but that time, I didn't know the answer. I wracked my brain trying to figure out what she could be asking me about a little chocolate chip cookie.

By that time, we had succeeded in drawing the attention of the entire restaurant so I was about ready to just give up. Instead, I thought I'd just take a chance. I answered, "Yes." I still didn't get my cookie. She took it around the corner and when she came back, she handed it to me. It was dripping with hot, melted chocolate.

Aha! I thought. *Now I know what she asked me, "Do you want your cookie warmed up?"*

I would much rather have not had it warmed up but by then I would have been happy to take it any way she gave it to me. I would even have taken the dough home and baked it myself.

After that, I got my revenge and I had a little fun, too. Whenever I ordered a cup of coffee, I didn't give the cashier a chance. I said, "I'd like a small cup of regular black coffee, without sugar, to go, please."

The reactions that I got were many. Some cashiers looked at me as though I was out of kilter. Some were caught by surprise and some thought it was pretty funny. I thought I was saving us both a whole lot of time and trouble.

Ordering a meal in a sit-down restaurant wasn't much easier but I was seldom alone so I always had help. But once in a while, when I wanted to feel independent or just plain spunky, I did my own ordering. I knew that there was a method to how an order is taken so I'm sure I got many a waiter or waitress rattled. I plowed right through without once looking up.

"I'd like the sirloin steak, well done, a baked potato and a garden salad with French dressing."

Invariably, I'd miss something like the onions or sour cream. I let Myron take care of that.

Other than the satisfaction of the meal itself, dining out wasn't all that enjoyable. In fact, had I still been thinking negative thoughts, I would have been a monster by the time the meal was over for most of the time I was alone with my thoughts.

It wasn't that I was being neglected, it was just too hard to try to keep up with the conversation. Often, I didn't even want anyone to attempt to talk to me unless they wrote me a note and that wasn't always practical.

So the evening when all the Tingelstads were out together up north, sitting around a table in a Chinese restaurant, I was content just to be there. But when my sister-in-law, Shirley, asked me, "Do you have a VISA card?" I was so happy to have understood her that I quickly answered "Yes."

"Do you like it?" she asked, to which I replied, "It's okay."

"Do you use it often?"

"Ho! Ho!, I think I use it too much," was my answer.

"Well," she said, "Now that we have grandkids, I thought it would be nice to have one."

Oh, Shirley, I thought, *You surely must be planning to spoil them.*

Then I began to think that I hadn't heard her correctly so I asked, "Shirley, what did you ask me?"

"Do you have a VCR?" she said.

It was but a month or two later that she and I began the exact same conversation but that time I caught on when she asked me, "Do you use it often?"

No, we don't have a VCR. She did buy one and I think they do use it often. I still have my VISA card and I still use that too often.

Show Grandma What You Want

One after another, Chuck, Ken and David were married. I wasn't able to hear the wedding music or their "I do's" with my ears but I heard them with my heart.

But after each ceremony, standing in the receiving line was one of the most difficult and frustrating things I had to do. I no more knew who the guests were after having been introduced to them than I did when they walked into the church.

The receptions were a bit more relaxing as then, when I found myself in a bind, I could take out my pad and pen. I'm sure Myron didn't mind that I wasn't pulling him out onto the dance floor but it really hurt me that I couldn't be there.

After being the only "Mrs. Weber" for so many years, it seemed at first, a bit odd to have daughters-in-law. But the boys chose wisely and we got along fine. I was able to read their lips fairly well and when I couldn't, they were receptive to writing notes to me.

Oh, there were times when we were all together that, in the hustle and bustle, I felt left out and the first little feelings of discontent would set in. But I never let them take root.

Then I would ask, "What are you talking about?"

Just knowing that would satisfy me so if anyone said, "Oh, nothing," they found out that it was the wrong thing to say to me. They learned quickly.

Myron and I had to wait a few years for our first grandchild. Jeffery Charles was born on May 20, 1993. That was one of the most joyful events of my life. I was finally a grandma and I took the role seriously.

I began to take care of him full-time when his mother, Sharon, returned to work eight weeks later. I wasn't afraid to take care of him and his mom and dad had confidence in me. But because I didn't want to slow down the progress of his speaking, I told them that I would give him up when he began to talk.

He was such a good baby and so easy and so much fun to take care of. He came early every morning with a big smile on his face and he left with it still there. It was a bit hard not to be able to hear him when he cried but I was always nearby. We set up a crib in my sewing room and he slept right through the clatter of the sewing machine as I sewed.

I had to "give-him-up" earlier than I had planned, though. During a craft sale, I injured my back and after that it was just too difficult to lift him. I couldn't, even then, give him up completely. He began coming every Friday.

Just as I had sensed that Papa could not hear me, I know that Jeffery knew that I couldn't hear him. When he was about two years old, Sharon explained to him and told him, "Look at Grandma when you talk to her."

Not only did he do that, he would stand as close to me as he could get, hold my face in his little hands, and jabber away. He carried that habit along with him when he was with his friends and, although it wasn't always a welcome gesture, it was so very, very cute to see him bent over talking to them.

Things changed between us as he got older. He was no longer content to get a smile or a "Yes" or "No" when he talked to me. He wanted Grandma to really talk to him. Sometimes he would just never give up. On a beautiful summer's day in 1995, we both reached our breaking point.

Jeffery loved to be outdoors so we were outside all morning. We played in the sandbox, we played basketball and we were then playing house. It was near lunch time so instead of eating our imaginary food, I asked him if we should have a picnic.

He looked at me, shook his head and said something that I couldn't understand. He said it again and I still couldn't understand. He wouldn't give up! Over and over he said it, until tears began to run down his little cheeks. By that time, I was crying, too.

That time I took his little face in my hands and told him, "Show Grandma what you want."

His face lit up into a smile and he took off. Up the steps of the deck he went as fast as his little legs could carry him. He pushed open the sliding glass door and went into the house.

Out he came with a even bigger smile on his face and a piece of paper in his hand. When he handed it to me and I saw what it was, I wanted to cry even more. His mom had put a McDonald's coupon in his bag and he wanted to go there.

You better believe that I didn't waste any time in getting us ready to go. I put him in his stroller and off we went up the street.

That was a major turning point in my journey. I was no longer content being deaf. I wanted to hear not only my grandson Jeffery but little Jacob who would be talking soon and I wanted them to be able to talk to their grandma.

Every evening, when Myron and I were eating supper, I would tell him that I wanted to find out if there was a powerful hearing aid that would help me. He finally gave in and made an appointment with a hearing aid dealership.

A couple of days before my appointment, he came home and told me that he had canceled it. I thought that he just did not have any hope of my being helped. But I was very wrong.

Instead, he wanted me to consult an ENT specialist. We considered returning to the Mayo Clinic but first he wanted to check into other specialists who were nearer to us. Not once did either of us even think of going to the University of Minnesota.

All winter we discussed it. Then, finally, he came home with the telephone number of Thomas A. Christiansen whose office was in the Unity Professional Building, only a few blocks from home.

Myron made an appointment for me but it would be spring before I could get in to see him. I was not yet ready for that trek of my journey. There was still a great deal for me to do before then but I could feel to the very core of my being that the answer was blowing in the wind.

PART EIGHT

LEAP OF FAITH

It was supper time when Dr. Levine, followed by his troops, fairly skipped into my room to release me. I found out then that my curiosity was still intact. Before he could leave, I timidly asked him, "Could you tell during surgery if I will be able to hear?"

He picked up a scrap of paper and wrote something and handed it to me. he watched me as I read, "No, we only tested the electronics of the device."

Dr. Levine must not have liked the look on my face. He picked up another scrap of paper, wrote something and with a smile, handed it to me. He had written, "It will work!"

When love and skill work together expect a masterpiece.

John Ruskin

Christmas Eve was especially nice that year. All the boys and their families came over in the afternoon. We all attended the early Christmas Eve church service and then returned home for supper. We hurriedly did the dishes and then gathered in front of the Christmas tree to open our gifts.

When all of our sons are together, there's a lot of bantering and joking back and forth. Kenny didn't want me to miss any of it. Before we began to open our gifts, he said, "Wait!" and went into the kitchen. He came back with a notepad and pen. All evening he kept me informed of what was being said by jotting down notes. I look at that as one of the most thoughtful gestures that anyone has done for me.

As usual, I received many nice gifts but there are two that stand out among the others. One was a television set with a remote control and built-in closed captioning which I received from Myron and the kids. The other was a ceramic pink pig or so I thought at the time. I didn't open the box. I laid it with my other gifts and planned to look at them all in the morning.

THE PINK PIG

I got up early the next morning. Myron, our son Scott and I were going to drive up to Pelican Rapids to celebrate Christmas with my sister, her friend Harold, and my brother Alvin. Before I began to get ready for the trip, I sat down to look at my gifts.

When I took the pink pig out of its box to set it on the coffee table, I saw that it wasn't an ornament after all. It was peppermint candy. There was also a little red hammer and a little story. I took time to read it. It seems the pig had special charms and those who broke it together with the little red hammer, on Christmas Day, would receive fortunes throughout the following year.

I'm not the least bit superstitious and other than wishing on my stars, I don't believe in lucky charms but it sounded like

169

fun so I decided to bring it with me up north and let the others share in the fun and a chance at receiving some good luck.

After the dinner dishes had been cleared, I placed the little pink pig in its pouch and we all gathered around the table. Each of us, in turn, took the hammer and gave it a whack. It shattered into bits and pieces.

We each picked a piece and ate it. It was the best peppermint candy I had tasted in a long time. I gave my sister a few pieces and put the rest in a plastic bag to take home with me, not for the fortunes that I expected to receive but for a good tasting piece of peppermint candy.

January 1997 arrived with record cold temperatures. It was so cold that no matter how much I bundled up, it was much too cold for my morning walks. I missed my McDonald's friends, Al and Bill, and I was also anxious to see the progress that was being made with the remodeling of the restaurant. All the antiques were going to be replaced with modern decor. There was one picture, that of an old wood-burning cookstove, that I liked and I was going to try to buy it.

By the end of the first week, I was about ready to climb the walls. When Saturday came, I had Myron drop me off. What a surprise I had! There wasn't any resemblance to the McDonald's of only a week before. All the shelves and the antiques that sat on them were gone. The walls were bare; the pictures that had brought back memories of my childhood were nowhere in sight.

When Myron came to pick me up, my friend, Bill, followed me out the door and motioned for me to go with him to his car. Quite often he would bring photos or other memorabilia to share with me so I thought that was what he was going to do.

First, he showed me the picture of an early 1900s grocery store that had hung on the wall of McDonald's. Then, much to my surprise and chagrin, he took out the picture of the old wood stove. Until then, I hadn't been too disappointed that I didn't get the picture. At least it helped not knowing who had it. Now, when Bill had it, I wasn't too happy. In fact, I was pretty jealous.

Then he handed it to me and said, "This is yours."

He had been in the restaurant the morning the pictures were taken down. He knew I had liked that particular picture and he got it for me.

Wow, I thought, *maybe the pink pig really is charmed and already I'm reaping the rewards.*

When the weather warmed up enough for me to resume my morning walks, I carried a bag of little pieces of pink peppermint in my pocket to share with Bill and Al. I certainly wasn't going to be selfish. I wanted them to have a chance at some good fortune too.

A few days later, I received a letter from a publisher of a proposed collection of poetry written in honor of mothers. At long last, I was going to have my work published and I was going to be compensated for it. I had submitted several poems and the two that were chosen were the ones I had written about my grandsons Jeffery and Jacob. If I had not heard from them by the end of February, I could assume that they would be included in the collection.

To what did I give the credit? The pink pig, of course! I kept right on eating him up and the fortunes kept right on coming.

One very, very cold day, UPS delivered a box from the Reminisce Company that was addressed to me. I hadn't ordered anything so thinking that Myron had, I set it aside.

But as the day progressed, so did my curiosity, until I couldn't wait any longer and I opened it. I found a book titled *We Made Our Own Fun* and an envelope that I assumed was the statement of the order. I didn't open it nor did I look at the book.

Something kept drawing me to that box until, finally, I went and looked again. This time I opened the envelope and read the letter. In essence, it read:

Dear Mrs. Weber,

Thank you for your contribution to *We Made Our Own Fun*. You will find your story on page —. Please accept this complimentary copy as a thank you.

It had been more than a year since I had sent in my submission of how Mama and Papa had met at the logging camp and it had completely slipped my mind. What else but the pink pig could bring me such luck? I kept on eating it and the fortunes kept right on coming.

Myron brought home a form from his office so I could enter the March Madness NCAA Basketball Tournament pool. I didn't know much about any team other than the Golden Gophers so I just checked off some teams at random. Then I sat up every game night to see if I had picked the winners. Of course, I had. I ended up tied for first place and my luck had even rubbed off onto Myron (he wasn't eating the pig) and he took second place. Together we won $180.

I was on such a roll that I even convinced him to buy a new car. I figured that our old '89 Ford had been at the mechanic's enough the past year. It didn't take him long to find what he wanted at the price he wanted to pay. He brought it home, drove it a couple days and brought it back. The pink pig had lost its charms.

GOD MEETS WITH THE ANGELS

I have often wondered just what God was thinking while all this was happening. I'm sure he must have been disappointed in me. So disappointed, in fact, that it's easy for me to imagine this scene taking place.

> *God calls a meeting with his angels, shakes his head and points his finger down to earth and says, "There's a woman down there that I am very displeased with. I have been giving her one blessing after another and who has she been giving the credit to? A pink pig! Can you imagine that?*
>
> *A pink pig!*
>
> *And just when I'm about to give her the most wonderful gift of all. I've had about enough of her shenanigans so before I give her that gift, we're going to have to straighten her out even if I have to put a scare into her. I certainly do not want a silly old pink pig to get the credit. I'll start out with something small and if that doesn't work, I'll have to resort to something more drastic."*

First, the poems I had written about my grandsons were returned along with a rejection slip. I had already told my sons and their wives so it was a big disappointment for them as well as for me. But that wasn't enough for me to lose faith in the pig. I continued to eat him and expected something good to happen any day. It didn't. Instead, things began to go downhill.

Wintz Trucking Company, where Myron was working, was going through a reorganization phase and it was uncertain whether or not there would be layoffs. He let the car go back.

Then, only a few weeks before my scheduled appointment with Dr. Christiansen, we got a notice in the mail that our group insurance coverage had been canceled. Not only for future claims but it was retroactive back to December 1995.

There were still a few pieces left of the pink pig. I ate them, no longer for the fortune I expected to receive but simply because it was good peppermint candy. I had come to my senses.

Myron didn't lose his job but he was no longer employed by Wintz. He was now employed by Dedicated Logistics, Inc., the name given the company after the reorganization.

Then, a week before I was to see Dr. Christiansen, Myron came home with a new health insurance card that I presented to a receptionist for the first time on March 5, 1996. It would be used over and over in the weeks, months and years to come.

I WANT TO HEAR MY GRANDSONS SPEAK

I was out of the soundproof booth of the ENT Professional Associates, Ltd. suite of the Unity Professional Building as quickly as I had been taken out of the operating room of Abbott Hospital so many years before. I hadn't heard a sound but even then I wasn't worried. I had a very strong feeling that there was something that could be done to help me.

On the walk up the hallway to the examining room where I was to meet Dr. Thomas A. Christiansen, I "heard" what that "something" was. As I stepped out of the booth, Lynne Barbatsis, the audiologist, said something to Myron that he related to me on a scrap of paper. "She said you may be able to have a cochlear implant."

By then, I was familiar with the phrase. In fact, a few years earlier my sister had done some investigating into it but I didn't have any idea just what was involved and I certainly hadn't thought it was for me. I had visualized it as being very compli-

174

cated and large but that didn't worry me. If I had to pull it along behind me in a wagon, and I could hear, I would gladly do so.

When Dr. Christiansen came into the room, he gave me a quick examination and then asked, "What is your motivation to hear again?" I didn't hesitate for a second. I replied, "I want to hear my grandsons."

He smiled and proceeded to tell us about the cochlear implant. He said that I had several things in my favor. I was able to speak and at one time, I had been able to hear. I knew there was a third but I could not remember what it was. I wrote him a letter to find out. He replied:

May 14, 1998

Dear Dora,

Your letter and the news of your project "Journey Out of Silence" is quite exciting. I will be anxious to read your work when it is completed.

When I first evaluated your ears and hearing on March 5, 1996, I was immediately struck by the contributions of very eminent ear surgeons on your behalf over the years. Clearly there had been definitive documentation of otosclerosis which, in your case, continued to progress. By the time I saw you, it was evident that you were relying on lip reading, and you were doing a very good job of that because audiometry suggested profound, essentially nonfunctional hearing in both ears.

I told you that complete deafness in both ears renders the suitability of considering a cochlear implant. This is particularly helpful to individuals who have not been born into the deaf world; rather, they miss dearly

175

the disconnect from aural-oral communication. You no longer could utilize a powerful but conventional hearing aid, and I also sensed that you were motivated to pursue alternatives. It was at that point that I knew referral to Doctor Sam Levine at the University of Minnesota would be of great importance to you.

You did me the extreme courtesy of coming back in January of 1997 so that I could witness the remarkable utility of your cochlear implant. My audiologist, Lynne Barbatsis who tested your hearing, and I couldn't have been more pleased. We are grateful for the resources of Doctor Levine and the University of Minnesota for the special needs of patients like you.

Sincerely yours,

Thomas A. Christiansen, M.D.

My motivation to hear my grandsons speak was good enough for him.

When he told us that he did not perform the implants and, instead, referred me to Dr. Samuel C. Levine at the University of Minnesota, I had a bit of deja vu. Not because I harbored ill feelings about the "U," as those had long since passed away but because of the aborted surgery of more than thirty years ago.

A Sound Decision

I had yet another month to wait before I could see Dr. Levine and I didn't spend it in worry. I had so strongly felt God's presence while I was with Dr. Christiansen that I was determined that my foolishness not come between God and me again.

In our mailbox the following day, there was a letter waiting for the mailman to take to Pastor Gary Galchutt at Prince of Peace Lutheran Church. I wrote that I was about to begin a journey to regain my hearing and invited him to come with me by way of prayer.

He was on our doorstep the day that he received my letter. His first question, written on a scrap of paper, wasn't, "Why do you want to hear?" He already knew why. Instead, he asked me "What is the doctor going to do?"

I didn't know much about the implant so I said, "He's going to make me hear!"

Then he wrote, "What is your doctor's name?"

I told him, "Dr. Sam Levine" to which he replied, "He's Jewish. You have a smart doctor."

He accepted my invitation to accompany me and wrote, "It will be an exciting journey." He prayed the first of many prayers for me that I could not hear and then said, "Good-bye" and left.

I began to pray, too. Very falteringly at first. Other than the "Now I lay me" that I had prayed when I was a little girl, "The Lord's Prayer," and our table prayers, I hadn't spent much time in prayer. I kept at it and it became easier and easier. Soon I was talking to God the same as I talk to my other friends.

I didn't bargain with him this time around. I bared my soul to him and I wasn't ashamed of the tears that ran down my cheeks. I let him know how hard it is not to be able to hear, how much I wanted to hear Jeffery's and Jacob's voices and how I wanted them to be able to talk to their grandma.

I told God that I wanted to hear the birds sing, to hear music once again and to hear a summer thunderstorm. And, yes, I took him at his word, "Therefore I tell you, whatever you ask in prayer, believe that you will receive it and you will."

Mark 11:24. I knew that I would hear again but just how well, I didn't know.

It had been several years since Myron and I had been on the campus of the University of Minnesota and many changes had taken place. The map that we had wasn't of much use, either, as there was road construction in the area with many detours. We were quite late by the time we found the Phillips Wangensteen Building that housed the ENT Clinic. We got later still as we wandered through the tunnels and hallways looking for the clinic.

Then when we did finally find it, we were told that we had to go back down to Out Patient Registration and get my red card. Even with all our tardiness, the receptionist and nurses greeted us with smiles and no one seemed to be frazzled.

I soon found out why. It was a busy place, a sure sign that their patients were being well cared for. Even with our delays, we had to sit and wait for quite some time before I was called in to see Dr. Levine.

In the course of my journey, I had seen ten doctors. No two were alike in stature nor were their personalities alike but the one thing they all had in common was their dedication to helping the deaf to hear. My doctor number 10, Dr. Levine, did not disappoint me. In fact, he did something that first day that none of the others had done which impressed me very much. He didn't speak to me through Myron. He "talked" to me.

He was handed a little TTY and he went to work. He first told me the history of the cochlear implant. I heard that the implants had been performed for several years worldwide before the first one was done at the University of Minnesota in 1985. He then explained how the implant was done and I heard once again that my bone growth might render the implant impossible to do. He took me through, one by one, the risks that were involved.

As he told me about each of the risks, dizziness, damage to my taste nerve and/or facial nerve and that I could lose my smile, Myron and I exchanged looks. He would then interject with "But maybe not." It was then that I sensed the confidence that he had in himself and I placed my trust in him.

As we were talking to Dr. Levine, Sharon Smith, the cochlear implant coordinator, peeked in and introduced herself. Her brilliant smile also won me over and I knew that I had come to the right place.

At the close of our visit, Dr. Levine turned me over to Sharon, in his words, to "Dot the i's and cross the t's." Just how many and how long it would take for her to do so, we did not yet know. My fortieth class reunion was coming up in July. Even though I wouldn't be able to hear, I had decided to attend. But, now that I would be hearing by then, it would be so much easier and fun! It didn't work out that way.

When Myron and I returned to our car, we were both unusually quiet and deep in thought. We hadn't driven far when we looked at each other and at the same time, began to say, "Maybe I (you) shouldn't...". Then I said, "N-a-a-a... ." He smiled and nodded his head, "Yes." We had made a sound decision!

THE LION'S TOUCH

Myron and I found the clinic easily the second time around and we arrived with time to spare. My eyes took in everything.

As we stepped off the elevator onto eighth floor, I noticed at the side of the entrance into the clinic, a sign that read "Lions International 5M Hearing Center." As we sat waiting for Sharon Smith, I noticed another sign posted near the receptionist's window, "The Story of the Lions 5M International Hearing Center." It read:

In 1972, help for the hearing handicapped was adopted as a major service of Lions Clubs International. A regional Multiple District Hearing Foundation was established to promote activities related to the hearing handicapped project.

In 1976, the Lions began raising funds for a capitol and building campaign for the Lions 5M International Hearing Center at the University of Minnesota. Over the next few years, a total of 1.7 million dollars was contributed by the Lions to help complete the clinic and research facilities.

The University of Minnesota Department of Otolaryngology gratefully acknowledges the contributions of the Lions and their continuing support of hearing research at the University.

Bob Nemeth at 1997 Cochlear Implant Picnic
Chair—Lions 5M International Hearing Foundation

Since my visit in 1978, the Lions had been very busy. They had picked up the clinic and carried it from the Mayo Building over to the eighth floor of the Phillips Wangensteen Building. They had done their job well.

There was now a spacious lobby with comfortable padded chairs. There was an amply furnished children's playroom and an abundance of friendly, smiley and helpful employees.

Along the walls was a display of plaques in honor of those who have contributed to the center. There were many but the ones that stood out prominently to me were Pelican Rapids, my hometown, and the town where I now live, Spring Lake Park.

There was something else on the wall that caught my eye. It was a large display case depicting the cochlear implant. It appeared to be much smaller than I had expected but yet even more complicated. When I read that some recipients compared the voices they heard to that of Donald Duck, I smiled as I remembered the early days of our married life when Myron entertained me with his perfect imitation of the famous duck. If that was what he would sound like, it would be good enough for me and in only a month, or so I thought, I would find out.

LAST RESORT

I can still see Sharon turn to me, that first day, as she opened the door of the soundproof room and say, "This is your last resort."

But now it doesn't seem like I was reading her lips. It feels like I heard her voice and that I always knew what her voice would sound like.

We were in the room for only a short while before Myron and I were taken to the Balance Lab where Andrea decorated me with electrodes and put me in a harness. She then led me into a little room where she strapped me securely into a high chair.

There I whirled and twirled in darkness and in light. I knew that the tests were needed for comparison should I have problems after surgery and I was shown flash cards with directions on what I was to do. However, other than finding out if I became dizzy, I didn't know what Andrea was doing behind the closed door.

I just relaxed and after a while, it actually began to be fun, especially trying to count backwards from 500 by 5s while being spun round and round in a pitch black room. If I wasn't going to be blasted off into space, I figured I was undergoing some pretty rugged space training.

After about an hour of that, we were back with Sharon. Using her computer, she filled us in with more information about the implant. Then she showed us the two devices. She didn't try to sway me into choosing either one. The decision was for me to make.

I am not mechanically minded so what I "heard" along those lines fell hard on my deaf ears. The microphone of the Nucleus was worn over the ear—much like an over-the-ear hearing aid. The microphone of the Clarion is contained in a single unit head piece. That simplicity is what appealed to me. I chose the Clarion. Nothing would be worn inside the ear.
Sharon said, "Your ears will only be for decoration."

It was then time for my visit with Dr. William N. Robiner, a senior psychologist at the University of Minnesota who works in tandem with the cochlear implant program.

When I learned that I was required to speak with him, my first thought was, *After forty-six years of being hearing impaired and deaf, I certainly don't need a psychologist to tell me if I could hear again. What foolishness! But,* I figured, *if that's what it takes, I'd better behave myself and cooperate.* I was apprehensive, too, wondering just what he would want to know and if my answers would satisfy him.

I really was nervous. I grew tense and my body broke out in a cold sweat. My mouth was so dry, it was difficult for me to talk. But talk I had to do. With the help of a computer, we talked for an hour.

I was beginning to find out just how important motivation was as his first question, too, for me was "What is your motivation to hear again?" My answer, "To be able to hear my grandsons speak," seemed to satisfy him also.

From there we journeyed back to my childhood, into adolescence, through high school, before marriage and right up to the present. I found myself opening up more and more to him as the session progressed so that I was sorry to see it end. By then my feelings towards a psychologist weren't quite so negative. He was really a pretty nice guy.

He gave me a questionnaire to fill out about my expectations of the cochlear implant and then he left to confer with Sharon. It was a tense time. I don't think Myron and I exchanged one word. I had been as honest as possible with Dr. Robiner. *Now,* I wondered, *would my honesty do me in?*

When he returned with a smile, I breathed a sigh of relief. He told us he didn't find any reason why I shouldn't have the implant. His last question for me was, "Will you be comfortable working with Sharon in the months to come?" That was easily and truthfully answered, "Yes."

He handed me his business card, shook our hands, and said, "Call me if you need me." I thanked him and though I told him I would, I was sure that I would not be needing him. How wrong I was!

When Sharon came back into the room and told me it was time for some audiologic testing, I found out that I wasn't going to escape the soundproof booth after all. When she clamped the headphone over my ears and told me to raise my hand when I heard a sound, I was puzzled. Then she left the room and sat down in the adjacent room with the familiar little window. *Then* it registered. I was in the soundproof booth!

Only it wasn't a booth. It was a spacious room with a desk, shelves that held toys, a TV set, computers and several chairs. It wasn't at all like the cramped little booths that I had sat in so many, many times.

There was something else very different, too. This time I didn't struggle to hear the sounds. This time I didn't want to hear them and I didn't.

All that was left to be done that day was to have a CT scan. But before that, I found out that I would not be hearing at my class reunion. Since the Clarion was not yet approved by the FDA, I would have to go through a series of speech and sound discrimination tests. We made an appointment and then went in search of the Radiology Department in the hospital.

After my CT scan, which was uneventful, we returned home, tired but hopeful, to wait for Sharon to call with the results.

WAITING AND PRAYING

During the ten years that I was deaf, my attendance at Sunday church services had fallen off drastically. It was not due to a lack of faith but rather to my noisy head. It was a no-win situation and I felt like I was being held under siege.

If I woke up to quiet conditions in the morning, by the time the service was half over the roaring would be back. My neck and shoulders would be stiff from tension. On the other hand, if my tinnitus was bad when I woke up, which was most of the time, I opted to stay home.

But from the Sunday following my visit with Dr. Christensen to the Sunday before my implant, I was in attendance regularly. It was a long, difficult hour. To make it go by more rapidly, I began to bring reading material along with me and if Pastor Galchutt noticed, he understood why.

I knew that a prayer for successful surgery went up to God that first Sunday only because Myron told me but what was said, I didn't know nor did it really matter.

It was then that I, not by my choice, became the center of attention. After the service, members of the congregation wanted to know what a cochlear implant was. This was something that very few, if any, had heard about. The question I was asked the most was, "Is it something new?" Thus began the first of my many mini-lessons even before I was told that I could have the implant.

That week of waiting for the results of the CT-scan was very long. I kept as busy as I could and oh, how I prayed. Even then, by the end of the week when I knew that Sharon would be calling Myron, I was a nervous wreck. As the clock ticked down the hours and then the minutes before he got home, I wanted to go and hide.

I couldn't read Myron's face when he walked into the den where I was watching TV. He was neither smiling nor was he unusually grim. He didn't say a word. He just handed me the note. It read: It wasn't possible to tell with the CT scan if there is fluid in your cochleas, so Dr. Levine has ordered a magnetic resonance image (MRI). I made an appointment for May 28.

All the pent-up emotions of the week of waiting threatened to come tumbling out and had the doorbell not rung, I know that I would have "lost it."

Myron opened the door and there stood Pastor Galchutt. He was dressed in work clothes, not in a suit that I had always seen him wear. He had been working in his yard, needed to run an errand, and since he was in the neighborhood, he thought he would drop in to see how things were going.

What perfect timing! So perfect, in fact, and so unprecedented that I know God had sent him. When I told him what had happened, he seemed to be every bit as awestruck as Myron and I. He didn't stay long, just long enough to pray and then he was gone.

That was the first of what I know were miracles I experienced during the following months. I know because things could not have just happened that way.

A couple days later, I began to experience pain and pressure in my right ear. I thought of calling the clinic but I was afraid Dr. Levine would find something wrong that would prevent me from having the implant. I confided in others—my back door neighbor and friend, Barb, and Myron. We were all mystified and also a bit afraid.

On the Sunday before Memorial Day, Myron and I drove up to Little Falls to meet my brother Herbert and his wife Lila for lunch. The pain and pressure were still there when we left and as we drove, something else happened. The pain and pressure subsided and that ear, which had always felt so plugged up, seemed to open up. I felt as though, at any time, I would be able to hear.

When we got home that evening, I asked Myron to look in my ear. He took the flashlight and peaked in. The only thing he noticed was that it was a bit red. The feeling of openness was still there the next morning and continued into the next day when I had my MRI. It has never felt plugged since.

Sis-in-law, Lila, me, Brother Herbert—1996
Little Falls Visit

WHATEVER WILL BE

The week spent waiting for the results of the MRI seemed to be only a little shorter than when I waited for the results of the CT scan.

Just like before, I managed to get through the first days easily. I sewed, worked in my flower garden and continued my morning walks to McDonald's. Towards the end of the week, trepidation had once more begun to creep in and it must have shown on my face.

I remember sitting, my head resting in the palm of my hand, so deep in thought that I was oblivious to what was going on around me. When I looked up, I was startled to find Gen, one of the employees, sitting across from me in my booth.

187

I had noticed her on previous visits but I had not become acquainted with her so I was a bit uneasy about speaking to her—afraid that I wouldn't be able to understand her.

I easily understood her first question, "What's the matter?" She asked it in what I would find out to be her caring and open manner. I opened up to her immediately and confided in her. I told her I was waiting to get the results of the MRI that would tell me whether or not I could have the cochlear implant. She was one of the few who was familiar with it. Each day after that, she met me with a smile and a word of reassurance.

But even then, by the end of the week, I was nervous and when Sharon hadn't called by Friday, I didn't know how I would survive until Monday.

Just like before when Myron came home from work on Monday, I couldn't read his face and I didn't want to read the note that he handed me. But when he refused to tell me what it said, I had no choice but to do so.

Tears of thankfulness flowed down my cheeks as I read:

> *"Left ear is filled with bone, won't work—right ear has fluid and will work. Sharon said it is maybe possible to have the Clarion model implanted but won't know for sure 'till Dr. Levine is in there. He will have both models with him in the operating room."*

Either one, the Clarion or the Nucleus 22 would be okay with me. I was confident that the one that was implanted would be the one that I was to have.

EPHPHATHA

I went to our church early the next morning to tell Pastor Galchutt the good news. He was very happy and I instinctively knew that my journey meant a great deal to him. I knew, too, that I would be welcome to talk to him at anytime. But I certainly did not expect to return only two days later. And certainly not in the condition that I was in, with tears running down my cheeks.

The tests, which were required by the Federal Drug Administration, had begun and I did not like it. My communication with Sharon had somehow broken down and my understanding of why the Administration needed the information was not at all the way my deaf ears heard.

Myron was with me, this time not only for support but because I needed him to be my ears. As sound and voices came from the speaker, he pointed to it and I had to guess what he was hearing.

After a multiple choice test of four written words, a noise or voice test and a sentence test came the "What do you hear test?" By then, I needed a diversion. I asked Sharon if I could be silly. She said, "Be as silly as you wish." I "heard" dogs bark, cats meow and lions roar. I heard cars, trains and airplanes, Donald Duck, Mickey Mouse and Pluto.

Then I grew tired of it and I began to think, *What if I'm lucky and get them right and the FDA won't let me have the implant?* The more testing I had to do, the angrier I became. Not at Sharon or the University of Minnesota but at the Federal Government. What right did they have to tell me whether or not I could have the implant? The next day I went to vent my frustrations unto poor Pastor Galchutt.

It was a very hot day so I must have looked a fright when I walked in, my face red and tears mixed with perspiration pouring down my face. Fortunately for him, Pastor Galchutt was out of his office. I was placed in the competent, though inexperienced, hands of Vicar Robert Mrosko. (A vicar in the pastoral field is the same as an intern in the field of medicine).

He gave me a cold glass of water and some tissue for wiping my brow. He had me pretty much under control by the time Pastor Galchutt arrived but I didn't get any help with the grievance that I had with the FDA. They weren't about to go head to head with the Federal Government. Instead, they each gave me a gift.

From Pastor Galchutt I received a little cross to carry in my pocket. Vicar Mrosko gave me this note:

Ephphatha - Hebrew Word
"Be opened." This is what Jesus cried to God when he
healed the mute man.
There is hope—Go for it!

On Sunday morning when I went to church, I also found this note in our church mailbox:

Dora,
I know that you said you haven't heard any of my sermons, but I do have typed manuscripts. If you would like copies to read, I would be glad to give them to you.
Vicar Mrosko

From then until he left to continue his schooling, I didn't have to bring my own reading material with me. Each Sunday I found a copy of his sermon and it was pure delight to know what he was talking about.

Unfortunately, he was gone before I had my implant. In the farewell letter I wrote, I thanked him for what he had done for me. I ended it with these words:

As I think about everything that has happened to me this past year, especially since my visit with Dr. Christiansen, I feel so strongly that God isn't just going to let me hear again. He has a plan for me and I am looking forward to finding out what that plan is.

TOUCHED BY AN ANGEL

I had renewed confidence and had even gained patience with the FDA. Myron had straightened me out about that. He explained that the FDA could not keep me from having the implant. The tests were needed to compare results before and after the implant surgery.

Good thing, too, as then I began the strenuous "tracking" sessions with Sharon Smith. The purpose was to evaluate my speech reception in a one-to-one situation, first by lipreading and then wearing my hearing aid.

I didn't have any worries there. I was a very bad lipreader and my hearing aid was of no use to me. What I didn't know was how bad I really was. I was given only one clue. That was the subject of the paragraph that she would be reading. After a sentence, clause or phrase, she would stop and I had to repeat word-for-word what she had said.

Even using the options of having her say it in a different way, repeating it or spelling certain words, we were unable to finish any in much less than a half hour. Some days I would become so frustrated that we would just stop and make an appointment for another day.

It was at the close of one such session that Sharon surprised me by telling me that I had to undergo yet one more audiologic test. Because my hearing loss was so profound, I needed to have a promontory stimulation test.

She gave me these words of assurance, "I have no doubt that you will respond."

An appointment was made for July 2. June, with its weddings and graduation open house celebrations, passed rapidly. If there was anyone who had not yet heard that I was going to have a cochlear implant, they found out then.

Most were excited and happy for me and shared my optimism but there were also the naysayers who said, "Don't get your hopes up too high." But I did have high hopes and I told them so. I hadn't come this far to let anyone rob me of my dream. The McDonald's Restaurant helped me keep that dream alive.

I began taking my walks early in the morning before it got too hot so at 6:30 there weren't many people up and about yet. Without Al and Bill to talk to, I had time to write lots of letters. But one morning something much more exciting happened that took my mind off any letter writing.

I was unaware that a man had sat down in the booth in front of me until I glanced up from my writing. Right away I thought, *With all the empty booths, why did he choose to sit right in front of me?*

Then when I noticed a cord on his neck, I wondered, *Could he have the cochlear implant?* I didn't think it possible but I kept looking and hoping he would turn his head so that I could see. When he finally did and I saw that he did have the implant,

I wanted to get up and hug him. Stranger or not, he wasn't going to get away before I could talk to him.

I went up to the counter on the pretense of getting a refill of coffee and stopped at his booth on the way back.

"Is that the cochlear implant?" I asked pointing to his head.

He said "Yes," but I sensed that he didn't wish to talk about it so I sat down.

But, of course, my curiosity got the best of me once again. I wrote a note and told him that I was going to be implanted and asked him where he had his and the name of his doctor. Of course, it was Dr. Levine at the University of Minnesota. That opened up the flood water gates.

He told me that he had lost his hearing with meningitis and had the implant that past December. He chose the Nucleus because he didn't want to wait as long as it would have taken to have the Clarion.

I was amazed at how well he could hear me and we got along well even though he had to write notes to me. After that, I would often find him waiting for me when I arrived early in the morning. It was like I was being touched by an angel and each time I felt more assured that I, too, would soon be hearing.

July arrived on a positive note. As Sharon predicted, I passed the promontory stimulation test easily. After that, I was so giddy with happiness that I was bumping up against the walls as I followed Sharon to the soundproof booth. Sharon and Myron were as happy as I was but there wasn't time to celebrate. We had more "tracking" to do.

We didn't get much done that day as my mind was not on what she was reading. She finally gave up and set up an appointment for a few days later.

Finally, I was given the date August 26 for my implant. Before I left that day, there was something I had to get off my mind. I told her about Eleanor and asked if she thought Eleanor could have the implant. Sharon answered, "Tell her to come down for an evaluation."

LET GO—LET GOD

*I listened motionless and still
And, as I mounted up the hill,
The music in my heart I bore,
Long after it was heard no more.*

William Wordsworth

I had loved and listened to music all my hearing years so I did carry many songs in my heart while I was deaf. Often I would wake up with one in my mind and it would remain with me for days. One of those times, it was, "It is No Secret," that played over and over.

During that time, Barb, my back door friend, came over carrying a pen and a pad of paper. She motioned me to come sit by the picnic table. What she told me was not good news.

Her husband, Kermit, was not well and had just come home from the hospital after undergoing testing. Internal bleeding showed up on the tests and he was to have more tests in the weeks to come.

During those days of our mutual waiting, the three of us had many talks while sitting at our picnic table. I shared that song with them and I will always remember the smile that lit up Kermit's face as he, too, recalled the words:

*"You may have longed for added strength
Your courage to renew
Do not be disheartened, for I bring news to you,*

It is no secret what God can do
What he's done for others, he'll do for you. . ."

Kermit was diagnosed with stomach cancer and underwent surgery in August, two weeks before my implant. More inoperable cancer was found. He passed away in April, 1997.

During the months after I regained my hearing, I visited with him several times. Even though things were not going well for him, he was happy for me and he marveled at how well I could hear. Although it is small, I do get some consolation in the timing of his death and the regaining of my hearing.

It is so much easier for Barb and me to converse even though she says, "You will put the paper companies out of business."

Myron and me with Chelsea Marie, our first grand daughter—1996

There was one other unhappy and very unexpected event that occurred while I was waiting. We received a letter informing us of Pastor Galchutt's resignation. His last Sunday at Prince of Peace was to be August 25, the day before my implant. *Would he,* I wondered, *have to rescind on his promise to be with Myron and me the day of surgery?*

Before I could get down to the church to find out, he was at our house with the assurance that he would be there. He also wanted me to know that although he would no longer be our pastor, he would continue to pray for a successful hook-up.

There were also several very happy and exciting things happening, too. My great-niece gave birth to twin girls, Shannon and Irelyn and Myron and I attended their baptism. We were presented with a granddaughter, beautiful little Chelsea Marie, on July 23. After our four sons and our grandsons, Jeffery and

Chelsea

Jacob, it was a very wonderful gift. I wasn't able to hear her cry but it wasn't quite so hard that time. I knew very soon that I would not only hear her cry but I would be able to hear her first words.

And I did, in the company of Myron, attend my 40th class reunion. It had been thirty years since I had last seen most of my classmates but,

Me and my friend Kenny—40th Class Reunion

even so, there were very few that I did not recognize. There was lots of hugging and tears flowing as we reminisced and I was not in the least bit uncomfortable that I could not hear them. It was a great evening that was even made better with my friend, Kenny, in attendance.

He was still just as nice and good-looking as I remembered and I did not have to resort to only staring at him. We had a nice little visit. I was happy to learn that he, too, is happily married and is the father of three children. And, yes, he was surprised and maybe a little proud, too, when I told him that I had a son named Kenneth LeRoy. He said, "That's my name!" I'm quite sure, too, that he believed me that LeRoy was named after my brother and not him.

I wasn't able to hear my classmates when they introduced themselves and that made me sad. When it came to my turn, I wasn't afraid. I had something wonderful to tell them.

Confidently, I stood up and said, "All my body parts, except my ears, are in excellent working condition and in only a few weeks, after my cochlear implant, they will work too. When we get together for our 45th reunion, I will be able to hear you all."

Of course, that little speech put the spotlight on me and for a time, I was the most popular girl in my class. I found out, too, that I had done a good job bluffing my way through high

197

school as there were many classmates who told me, "I didn't know that you couldn't hear."

I was surprised when a classmate told me that his friend works in the manufacture of cochlear implants and that he was working on an ear level model. Unless there is yet a third model, it is quite possible he was referring to the Nucleus ear level device that will soon be available to the public.

In the meantime, the FDA had made the decision to approve the use of the Clarion Model and Sharon called with the news a few days before my implant. I would like to be able to write that the hours I spent with Sharon helped in their decision but I can't. The results of my tests were a bit late in helping them but they certainly were not useless to me.

I learned to be patient but, best of all, I had the chance to work with Sharon and to become better acquainted with her. It would have been so much more fun and a whole lot easier the second time I had the tests but it was okay, too, to know that there would be a great deal fewer that I would have to do.

I had one more visit with Pastor Galchutt before my implant. The advice he gave me, "Let go - let God" and "Regress back to your childhood and pretend that you are taking a nap for your mama," would be easy to do and it will stay with me forever.

It Will Work

On August 26, 1996, Myron and I were on our way to the University Hospital at 4:30 a.m. From the time I arrived to the time when I was wheeled into the operating room, everything went like clockwork.

When Sharon arrived, I had Myron and Pastor Galchutt by my side and I was about ready to go into the operating room. She asked, "Are you afraid?"

I smiled, pointed to Pastor Galchutt and said, "No, I have my pastor with me."

The last thing I remember before I left the pre-induction room was seeing Pastor Galchutt, his hands folded, his eyes tightly closed and his head bowed in prayer.

As his 98th cochlear implant patient, Dr. Levine began his work. Four hours later I woke up in the recovery room. The next time I woke up, I was being wheeled into my hospital room. I woke up only long enough to say a quick "Good-bye" to my brother, Herbert and sis-in-law Lila, who had been with Myron during surgery and then I was sound asleep once again.

I woke up briefly when Dr. Levine came to check on me and tell me that he had put in a Nucleus. A while later, Sharon came and explained why. This is what she wrote:

> *Dr. Levine has to use a special surgeon's tool with the Clarion. He threaded a "dummy" implant into the tool and inserted that into your cochlea. He hit a blockage and the dummy wire bent. He was not able to get full insertion. With the tool, it was hard for him to feel whether the block was simply difficulty with the wire or a block in the cochlea.*
>
> *The Nucleus is hand-fed into the cochlea and, therefore, easier to feel any resistance and move accordingly. He inserted the Nucleus, felt a block, and moved the wire. The resistance gave way and he got full insertion.*
>
> *Had he gone with the Clarion, the wire (electrodes) would have been crimped and only in part way. You likely would not have received as much information as you will with the full insertion of the Nucleus.*

I wasn't at all disappointed not to have the Clarion implanted. I knew I had what I needed and that Dr. Levine had it safely tucked away in the recesses of my head.

I hadn't given any thought as to whether or not I had lost my taste or my smile. When David and Allison came that evening, that was the first thing they wanted to know. My supper sat untouched. Allison put something on the fork and told me to taste it. I did and I said, "Yuck!" She laughed and then I laughed. Neither was I dizzy or nauseated nor did I have much pain. I was in tip-top shape but very, very tired.

By noon of the following day, I was up walking in the hall and trying to visit a young man named Michael who also had been implanted the day before. But, alas, he was sound asleep so I didn't get to meet him until after he was hooked up.

It was supper time when Dr. Levine, followed by his troops, fairly skipped into my room to release me. I found out then that my curiosity was still intact. Before he could leave, I timidly asked him, "Could you tell during surgery if I will be able to hear?"

He picked up a scrap of paper and wrote something and handed it to me. He watched me as I read, "No, we only tested the electronics of the device."

Dr. Levine must not have liked the look on my face. He picked up another scrap of paper, wrote something and with a smile, handed it to me. He had written, "It will work!"

JACOB
A CHAT WITH GRANDMA

Where did you come from, Jacob Dear?
I came from someplace between there and here.
What did you do while you were there? Did you have fun; did you have good care?
I climbed on rainbows and I caught falling stars. I bounced on clouds and put moonbeams in jars.
How did you get here, Jacob Dear?
On a wing of an angel, who was so fair.
Why did you cry when you got here. Did you think you had so much to fear?
I saw my angel disappear. But I soon knew that I need

not fuss because Mommy and Daddy loved me so much.

How did your skin get so soft, Jacob Dear? And where did you get your pretty hair?

I played in a sandbox filled with angel dust; and the sun burned my hair a little too much.

Where did you get your eyes so bright, your happy grin and teeth so white?

They came from Mom and Daddy one cold and wintry night. Don't you think on me they look just right?

How did your legs get so sturdy and strong so that you could walk before you were one?

Silly question, Grandma, for if you don't know, you surely should. It's because I ate all my angel food!

> *With Love,*
> *Grandma Weber*
> *April 1995*

JEFFERY

The first time that I saw you, Jeffery, you lay cradled in your mother's arms. Though you were only a half hour old, you possessed so many charms. I wasn't at all surprised to see you were so cute, cause you had your daddy's dimples and your mommy's sparkling eyes. Your tiny nose was white and flat; your hair was thin and fair.

You didn't seem to miss a thing; you were looking everywhere. Your eyes, they were wide open and I know that you could see, cause when I took you in my arms, you looked straight up at me. When you heard your daddy's voice, your head turned way around, for that to you had already become a very familiar sound.

Now you are almost one year old—you sing, you talk, you dance. You like to crawl and stand and laugh; you very seldom cry. Your eyes turned brown just like your mom's. Your smile is very broad. You're getting teeth and lots of hair, you have dimples everywhere. You bring to me a lot of joy while I take care of you and in the many years to come, you'll bring me more, Grandson.

With love,
Grandma
March, 1994

PART NINE

BEYOND THE SILENCE

Sharon looked at me with a questioning smile and asked, "Are you ready?"

I answered "Yes," and with a flick of a switch, I came to the end of my journey out of silence. Myron spoke and I heard. In no way was I prepared to hear as marvelously as I did. Donald Duck had stayed at home in Disneyland.

I don't think of all the misery, but of all the beauty that still remains.

Anne Frank

The affects of the anesthesia were slow in leaving. I spent most of the next forty-eight hours sleeping, only waking half-way to visit with friends and relatives who stopped in. On Wednesday evening, my daughter-in-law, Allison, came to wash my hair and check the incision.

Allison is a certified Medical Assistant so I felt pretty smug having my own private nurse. I was still very tired so I let go and let her competent and soothing hands work their magic. Soon I was sound asleep, my head resting on the table.

Friday, the 30th, was my 58th birthday. Pastor Galchutt brought me a lovely mum plant and Chuck, his wife Sharon and little Jeffery, who thought I had been away from McDonald's long enough, brought me a Big Mac, fries and a chocolate shake.

Of course, since his mom and dad had told him that the doctor was going to fix Gramma's ears, Jeffery expected me to hear him that day. He thought I should play with him, too, but after only a short try, I gave out and crawled back into bed.

That first week went by rapidly and I was fully recuperated when I returned to the clinic to have the staples removed. Dr. Levine said the wound was healing nicely but told me not to put the bow of my glasses on so as not to irritate it. Then, before he left the examining room, he wrote me this note:

"You are finished with the surgeon. Now the hard part starts. You have to learn how to use the thing. If you have any problems you can call me on the telephone."

Those three little lines spoke volumes. I knew that Sharon would be "hooking" me up and that I would be working with her for several months so I understood the part about being finished with the surgeon, and I found it quite amusing that he called the device "the thing." It was the rest of the message that puzzled me.

I hadn't allowed myself to think beyond just being able to hear; I didn't dwell on what things would sound like or how much I would hear. When I read Dr. Levine's, "You can call me on the telephone," I thought he was being overly optimistic. But it was the words, "Now you have to learn how to use the thing," that both puzzled and frightened me.

If after two years, I still hadn't learned everything there is to know about operating our new vacuum cleaner, how in the world would I get the twenty-two electrodes and the receiver that I now had in my head, to work with the transmitter and the sound processor that I would soon get? I didn't communicate my fears to Myron but I made a mental note to make sure he listened when Sharon explained it to us at "hook-up."

I didn't follow Dr. Levine's advice about the bow of my glasses and I put it back on my glasses before the incision was healed properly. With each of her visits, Allison became more concerned that the wound was becoming infected. Myron was concerned, too, and he began putting more and more ointment on it. Finally, on a Saturday, Allison thought it best to check with Dr. Levine.

Dr. Boyer, a resident who had assisted with the implant, was on call. She gave us a choice of either going to ER at the University Hospital or to our family doctor. Unwisely, I chose to see our family doctor and we found out just how unknown the cochlear implant is, even in the medical field.

The first doctor who came into the examining room didn't want anything to do with it and stayed an arm's length away. Neither did the second doctor want to treat it and he told us that we should have returned to ER at the University Hospital.

Finally, after a lengthy visit, a third doctor came in. He, too, was unfamiliar with the cochlear implant but he did show an interest and he was helpful. He said Myron had been applying too much ointment and the wound was unable to "breathe." All the while that he was cleaning it, I sat in mute attention, watching Myron and Allison as they educated him on the workings of the cochlear implant.

Thus it was, just as it had been since my first visit to the Audiology Clinic at the University, that things continued to go against the norm and I did have to return to see Dr. Levine. By then the wound had healed but he still cautioned me to leave the bow off my glasses. That time I listened to him. He also told me that he wanted to look at the wound again when I returned for "hook-up" which was only two weeks away.

Those two weeks went by rapidly. I did the handwork on the Barbie clothes that I had sewn before the implant, I visited neighbors and friends and I resumed my morning walks to McDonald's. There I found Jerry, my implant friend, waiting to inspire and encourage me.

I went shopping for a new wardrobe, too. I could either wear the processor in a pouch clamped to my jeans or in a pocket. I chose to carry it in a pocket. I purchased several pocket T-shirts in every color of the rainbow and some shirts to wear over them. One was green with long sleeves. It, too, had pockets and peeking over them were Walt Disney characters. Without a thought to the Donald Duck connection, that was the one I wore to my "hook-up" appointment.

BLESSED ASSURANCE

I was awake early that morning and was dressed and ready long before Allison was to pick me up. Myron had gone on ahead of us so as to get in a few hours at work. He said he would meet us at the clinic. He was there waiting for us when we walked in.

Sharon Smith and me

While we waited for Sharon, we had a surprise visit from my angel, Jerry, who had come over from McDonald's. He didn't stay long—just long enough to wish me luck and then he was off to work in the Cochlear Implant Research Lab at the clinic.

Soon after, Sharon walked in, her arms laden down with boxes. I thought, *What is all that? Maybe I will need a wagon to pull it in, after all.*

She said, "Let's go," and we followed her to the little room that had become my home away from home. Sharon opened the boxes, one by one, and laid the contents on the table. Each part, the speech processor, microphone, cords and transmitter, was in its own container. Then she began assembling all the parts.

It looked very complicated to me and I remember asking Myron, "Are you paying attention?"

He thought I was joking but I certainly was not. When she had finished with the assembly, I was amazed at how compact "the thing" was. It reminded me very much of a Walkman and I certainly didn't need anything but the pocket of my T-shirt and my head on which to carry it.

Then she placed the microphone over my ear and began moving the transmitter, with its attached magnet, around on the side of my head, looking for the receiver with its magnet that was implanted inside my head. After a few minutes, she leaned over, looked me in the face and said, "I can't find it."

While washing my hair, I had felt a bump near the site of the incision and pointing up there, I asked her, "Is it up there?"

She laughed and said, "No, it's not way up there!" With that she left the booth, saying, "I'll be right back."

All sorts of thoughts came to me. I had tried not to sleep on that side after surgery but since it's my favorite, I often woke up on that side. *Maybe,* I thought, *I had jarred it loose and it had moved or perhaps Dr. Levine might have forgotten to implant it.*

By then it was nearing 10 o'clock and Allison had to leave for work. She missed a very prodigious event.

Sharon returned, adjusted the outside magnet and it grasped the implanted magnet on the first try. I expected her to put a battery in my processor and I would be done. There was much more involved than that. Instead, she plugged the processor into her computer and said, "Let's get to work."

She handed me this handwritten note, "Don't worry if you don't hear anything right away. It may take five minutes."

Sharon turned her computer on and I heard a sound immediately. She gave me a questioning look and asked, "Do you hear that?" I assured her that I did and she shrugged her shoulders and said, "Okay." She continued to slowly but steadily increase the loudness until I was comfortable with the level. She did the same with each electrode.

All went well through the first few and then something she had told me might happen, did begin to happen. For the next few minutes, eight electrodes, one after another, caused my face to twitch or made me dizzy and they had to be shut down.

Sharon assured me that I wouldn't need them so I wasn't too alarmed but, believe me, when I was able to take the ones that were remaining right up the scale, I was pretty relieved.

There were more steps to the "hook-up" process that involved balancing the loudness of the electrodes. When I thought everything was balanced, Sharon disconnected the processor from her computer and placed a battery in the battery compartment.

Sharon looked at me with a questioning smile and asked, "Are you ready?" I answered "Yes," and with a flick of a switch, I came to the end of my journey out of silence. Myron spoke and I heard. In no way was I prepared to hear as marvelously as I did. Donald Duck had stayed at home in Disneyland.

Outside the Soundproof Booth

The first few minutes that I spent beyond the silence are a complete blur. I don't remember getting up off my chair but the first thing I remember is that all three of us, Sharon, Myron and I, were standing together on Sharon's side of the table.

Sharon asked me, "What does Myron's voice sound like?"

I answered, "Exactly the way I remember it to be."

Then I started to laugh. I couldn't believe how loud my own voice was and I kept asking, "Is that my voice?" They both laughed and assured me that since no one else was in the booth, it had to be mine.

Then Sharon asked me, "What does my voice sound like?"

My answer, "Like a Norwegian," made Myron and her laugh even more. When she said, "I'm not Norwegian. I'm French and English," I realized my mistake. What I had meant to say was, "A typical Minnesotan." But that wouldn't have been right either and she would have said, "I'm not from Minnesota. I'm from Upstate New York."

She wasn't finished with me yet, however. She looked at me with a puzzled expression and asked, "How do you know what my voice sounds like? You haven't heard it before."

Without missing a beat, I answered, "If Myron's voice sounds like Myron's voice, then your voice sounds like your voice."

I think that convinced her that I, indeed, was hearing marvelously well! I was able to hear all her instructions—how to place the battery in the compartment, how long to expect it to last, and how to recharge it. She told me to be sure to place the device in the "dry pac" every night and then she explained the controls.

The more she explained, the more comfortable I became and it no longer seemed to be so formidable. I actually began to think that I could learn to operate it. When she gave me the manual and told me that it was my homework to read before returning the following morning, I believed her and fully expected to be given a quiz.

Then it was almost time to leave but before we left, she told me what to expect when I stepped outside the soundproof booth. She said it would be very noisy. The waiting room would be nothing but a hubbub of noise. The elevators would make a racket, the toilets in the ladies' rooms were powerful and when I stepped outside the building, I would be up against the worse din of all.

She was correct on all four counts. The waiting room was a cacophony of sound—children crying and playing, patients talking and telephones ringing. The elevator sounded like a freight train, I thought I would be flushed down the toilets and the street sounds made my head whirl. But she was wrong about some things.

She said Myron and I would not be able to converse while driving home. She showed me a little microphone that might help. I could plug it into my processor and he could speak into it as I held it up to him.

We chatted all the way home without the help of the microphone. He didn't have to face me, either, something that I always thought distracted him from his driving.

I was not expected to be able to utilize the car radio but I was able to pick up parts of what the announcer was saying and music already sounded good to me. It was so resonant that I could distinguish, during an instrumental, between the different instruments even though I could no longer remember their names.

When we got home, the telephone rang and I recognized it immediately. Myron rang the doorbell. I didn't hear it from the kitchen. I went into the living room and I heard the familiar ding-dong. Today I hear it from any room in the house.

I had never heard the sounds of the microwave so he introduced me to those. Then I understood why he covered his ears at the final b-e-e-e-p!

I know that Myron would have liked to have stayed home with me that afternoon. He was having as much fun as I was but he had to return to work. My fun continued.

SILENT NO MORE

One beautiful spring day when Chuck was two years old, we took a ride up to Pelican Rapids to visit Grandpa and Grandma Tingelstad. Four hours was a long time for an active little guy like him to sit still. When we drove into the driveway, I opened the door and set him free. Off he ran across the meadow.

Grandma probably had been sitting by the window all morning watching for us. When she saw us, she came outside.

She wasn't interested in Myron and me. She was laughing and watching Chuck. I will always remember the words she spoke, "He's like a little calf who is let out of the barn for the first time in the spring."

Those words best describe how I felt when I regained my hearing. I wanted to run and kick up my heels or to shout out the good news from our roof top but I'm not demonstrative so, instead, I went from neighbor to neighbor.

It seemed that everyone was giving me something to hear. One neighbor was out in his garden with his roto-tiller and several were mowing their yards. My back door neighbor, Barb, was calmly sitting by her picnic table waiting for me to come home. I walked over and above the din of the lawn mowers and roto-tiller, we talked and laughed and cried.

Oh, I didn't like the quiet of the house when I went back in. Just to hear sounds, I opened and shut the cupboard doors because they squeaked, ran the water, turned the microwave on and, unnecessarily, cleared my throat over and over again. When I had enough of that, I stood on the front door step and listened.

I could hear a car coming down the street long before I saw it and I heard car doors shut but couldn't see the cars. I heard the kids at my neighbor's Day Care as they played outside and I heard one incessant sound over and over. But no matter how hard I tried to figure out what it was, I couldn't.

The most surprising of all the sounds that I had heard that day came to me when I was making supper. I can laugh now when I think about it but at the time I didn't find it to be a bit amusing. Sharon hadn't warned me about that one.

I fried bacon for BLT sandwiches. The bacon sputtered and crackled, snapped and hissed. I actually thought we had bought a bad package of bacon and that I better get away from it before it began to fly out of the frying pan. I went and stood in the living room. The sputtering died down and when I got my courage up, I returned to the kitchen. Myron came home to some crisp and very dry bacon on his sandwiches.

As all this was taking place, memories of one other frightening incident came to my mind. That one happened when I was a little girl and home alone.

I was working on a project for school that required some pasting and I didn't have any paste. Mama had often made some for me using flour and water so I thought I could easily make some by myself. When I opened the flour bin, I didn't find any flour.

That's okay, I thought, *I'll use baking soda.*

I put some in a bowl and added water. It wasn't thick enough so I added more baking soda. The consistency was improving but then I saw something else. It was beginning to bubble. I put more soda in and it bubbled more and soon it was climbing out of the bowl. That was enough of that. I opened the door and I threw it, bowl and all, as hard and as far as I could down the hill. My project went unfinished and I have never tried making my own paste since—not even with flour.

I didn't turn the closed captioning (CC) off when we sat down to watch the evening news. I didn't want to know, yet, if I could be without it. I had already received so many surprise gifts that I wanted to save one to open later. But I did discover that I was able to hear and understand the voice of the anchor easily as I followed along on the CC. I also found out that what the anchor said was often much more interesting than the words of the captioning. When the weather came on, I wasn't upset that it wasn't captioned. I knew what the forecast was without it. I understood the weatherman very well.

Later that evening, I had yet another surprise while watching TV. Besides being colorful, the wheel on *Wheel of Fortune* is noisy with the sound of bells going off when a correct letter is called.

By then I was tired and my brain, which hadn't worked that hard for many, many years, must have been, too. I did as Sharon had suggested. I took "the thing" off. I was plunged back into silence and I did not like it! I couldn't wait until morning so I could put it back on. I wonder if I knew then that I wouldn't be able to put it on in the morning if I would have slept with it on.

Can She Hear the Birds?

I was up even earlier the next morning. I hurried to wash my hair and get dressed. I couldn't wait to hear again. But I didn't get to even turn the processor on. Just as Sharon had the morning before, I had a problem getting the two magnets to grasp each other.

Oh, boy, now what, I thought.

I tried and I tried. Myron tried and tried but to no avail. I burst into tears, put it in the dry pac and carried it with me to the clinic.

Sharon came into the waiting room, spun her magic and with the first try, the magnets grasped. She flipped the switch of my processor and I was once more "on the air." Then we were off to have Dr. Levine check the wound.

Before he came into the room, Dr. Boyer took out her scissors and clipped the hair that had grown over the receiver. My hair is thick and that, she explained, was interfering with the magnets. That problem still remains and every two weeks I have to cut it. She was finished before Dr. Levine came and I was again hearing marvelously well.

217

I will always remember the first words I heard Dr. Levine speak. When Sharon informed him that I could hear, he smiled and asked her, "Can she hear the birds?"

Sharon wasn't about to answer for me. She looked at me and said, "Do you?"

I didn't know if I had or not so I said, "I don't think there are any song birds still around."

Later, I remembered the incessant sounds that I had heard the day before and I was pretty sure that it had been the singing of the birds. It had been a very long time since I had heard them. So long, in fact, that I don't ever recall hearing them. I do remember the time about twenty years ago when I couldn't.

It was a beautiful early Sunday morning in the summer. There are lots of trees in our back yard that attract birds of all kinds such as robins, sparrows, Baltimore orioles, finches, cardinals and others. Chuck was sitting out on the deck and I went to join him. He told me that he was listening to the birds. I looked around and I could see them everywhere and I could tell they were singing but I could not hear them. Now, wonder of wonders, I could hear them.

When I got home that afternoon, I stood on the deck and listened. Sure enough, I heard the same sound over and over. I couldn't see any birds but I was quite sure, then, that was what I had been hearing. I received firm confirmation later in the day when I decided to walk up to our church.

On the walk I kept hearing the same sounds but again the birds hid from me. I guess they all wanted to greet me at once. As I walked, the sound became louder and louder and when I reached the church yard, I saw them. The ground was covered with a flock of blackbirds, magnifying the sound I had been hearing, a hundred times over. I would hear other birds with a much more beautiful song but, that day when I heard them, nothing could have been more beautiful.

When I walked into the church office, I expected to surprise Jan, our church secretary, who also had given me much encouragement. She had gone home and a young girl named Julie was at the desk. We talked for an hour. Then she said, "I think we should go and talk to Mrs. Galchutt."

Mrs. Galchutt is a teacher at Prince of Peace Day School. It was recess time and we found her sitting at her desk. Myron had called Pastor the previous evening with the news that I could hear at "hook-up". What he didn't tell him was just how well I could hear. We wanted to surprise him. Now when Mrs. Galchutt saw me, she became so excited that she took out her cell phone and called him immediately. He said he would be over to see me that evening but his visit had to be put on hold for 24 hours. I was once again plunged back into silence.

When I got home from my visit to our church, I went out to the mailbox to get the mail. Just then an extra loud car went by. Coincidence or not, my right eye began to twitch so badly that I had to take my "thing" off. By the time Myron got home, I was in tears. He immediately called Sharon and she told us to come in the next day.

She was waiting for us and soon found the guilty electrode and shut it down. Again she assured me that I didn't need it. I was then down to my present thirteen.

I had one more appointment that week but that day I was on my own. Myron told me, "You don't need me to hear for you anymore," and dropped me off at the door of the Phillips Wangensteen Building.

I was like a child who buys her own candy bar for the first time. Confidently, I walked up to Lelo, the receptionist at the clinic, handed her my red card and told her that I had an appointment with Sharon.

What a thrill it was to be able to answer, "No, I will be picked up," when she asked me, "Do you have a parking ticket for me to stamp?"

Gramma Can Hear Me Now!

It was Scott, our youngest son, who picked me up. Of all the boys, I think he was the least surprised that I could hear again. He had never liked writing notes to me and did so only as a last resort. We could now converse without any problem. But he wasn't satisfied with that. He wanted me to hear everything and he began on the drive home.

He worked the radio, switching from one station to another, all the while asking, "Can you hear that?" Whenever a song was playing that he thought I would remember, he would say, "You know that one." I would listen and, sure enough, I would recognize it. One such song was the Everly Brothers singing "Bye Bye, Love." I was able to understand the words and it was far richer than I ever remember it being.

Sharon, Chuck's wife, and Jeffery were parked in our driveway when we got home. Sharon, too, was filled with awe when Jeffery said, "Let's go play, Gramma," and I answered, "Okay." She left us alone together for the afternoon so Jeffery could get to know his new Gramma. What a wondrous time it was.

Jeffery was shy at first and still looked at me when he talked to me. But once he caught on that I really could hear him, he wouldn't stop talking. He didn't let me get away with my "Yes" or "No" answers, either; he demanded that I explain myself. Then my battery went dead so I had to show him just how the "thing" worked.

After that, if he asked a question and I didn't answer right away, he would ask me, "Do you have your battery on, Gramma?"

When Sharon picked him up, we were both all smiles. When I told her how wonderful Jeffery's voice sounded, he looked at her, the biggest smile on his little face, and said, "And Gramma can hear me now."

OH, GIVE ME A HOME

Chuck stopped in that evening on his way home after work. He always comes wearing a smile but that day it was bigger and brighter than ever. All he could say as he, his dad and I sat on the couch and I was able to follow along with the conversation was "Unbelievable!"

Kenny's reaction was much the same, only his remark was a bit different. Over and over, he repeated, "It's unreal!" Janine responded with a smile and lots of questions, just to see if it was real. Chelsea had the honor of being the first grandchild I heard cry and Jacob was the first I heard sing. He sang a song that he had learned in Day Care and one that I knew well, "Home on the Range."

I didn't hear much, though, only "Oh, give me a home, where the buffalo roam," because by then I was both laughing and crying.

Allison was very happy but she just kind of accepted it without questions. David's remark was the best of all, "Mom, I think you've been fooling us and you have been able to hear all along."

On Saturday, I went to visit more neighbors. The news was met with hugs, smiles and, very often, tears. While I was talking with Sandy in her garage, she said, "Do you hear that noise?"

Ann and me

I listened and yes, I did hear something but I didn't recognize what it was. Then I knew.

"It's a train whistle," I said. It certainly was and I heard it from a distance of one mile.

One of my neighbors, Carol, had a special interest in the cochlear implant. She knew Ann, a little three-year-old girl, who lived in Oakton, Virginia who was deaf. She said she would tell her parents about the cochlear implant.

But her parents did know about the implant. They just had not yet made the decision. After hearing, through Carol, of my success and seeing the results of others, they decided to pursue it.

Ultimately, and unplanned, little Ann had the implant on August 26, 1997, at Johns Hopkins University Hospital in Baltimore, Maryland, exactly one year after I received mine. Ann, with the devoted attention of her parents who give her daily speech therapy, is making great progress.

I had the pleasure of meeting Ann and her daddy and her grandma this summer. At that time, her daddy told me, "The eloquence of some of the sounds that she can produce is a pleasure to listen to and some of the sounds that she is responding to, I am not sure that I can hear."

Shout of Acclamation

It was a busy week but I wasn't finished yet. I still had to go to McDonald's to tell my friends. As though it was today, I can still see Al poke Bill and point to me as I came in the door. I'm sure that they could tell by my smile what they were about to witness. When they began to talk to me and I responded, their faces showed both wonder and gladness.

We chatted for quite some time, never once having to resort to writing notes. But for some reason, I missed those "love notes" then and I still do. It just isn't the same without them.

When we walked into church on Sunday, I was immediately surrounded by members of the congregation. They, too, were awed by the success of the implant but they also wanted to see the device and to hear just how it worked. I finally just took it off and left it off until I had satisfied all who were interested.

We have a beautiful pipe organ in our church with the pipes installed on the wall in the back of the church. That was where we sat that first Sunday. I wasn't at all expecting it to be that loud but now, when I think about it today, I think of it as God's triumphant shout of acclamation. It was so loud that I had to hold the magnet away from my head until the hymn was over.

I wasn't yet able to understand the words of the sermon but I certainly did hear Pastor's voice and for the first time in many years, I was able to follow along and participate in the liturgy. Then, with tears blurring my eyes, I heard Pastor as he prayed, thanking God for restoring my hearing.

The week was coming to an end and what a glorious week it had been. I felt blessed beyond measure and I didn't need anything more. But there was more to come before it drew to a close. We heard the words that we had been waiting to hear since the loss at birth of Chuck and Sharon's little Jennifer Marie two years before. It was a secret that they had been keeping from us until I could hear Jeffery say, "We're going to have a baby!"

Hold the Line

The next few months were filled with even more wonderful things. I hadn't seen any of my crafter friends since I had begun my cochlear implant evaluation so I took them by complete surprise at the first craft sale that fall.

I only had to tell one crafter, my friend, Nancy, and the news spread on down the line like wildfire from one crafter to another. There was a great deal of rejoicing in crafter land that weekend. Crafters stopped by with good wishes and a great deal of curiosity and, once again, I found myself explaining the wonders of the Nucleus 22 Channel Cochlear Implant System.

And, oh, how great it was to be able to chat with my customers and to hear the comments of passersby, even the negative ones. The first comment was from a little girl. She said, "I'm too old to play with Barbie but I like your clothes anyway. They are the prettiest that I have ever seen!"

We made a trip up north so my brothers and sister could talk to me. While we were there, I had the opportunity to have lunch with a few of my classmates. We had such a great time; our laughter became contagious and soon other patrons were laughing right along with us even though they didn't have any idea what we found to be so funny. I think, though, that had we not left when we did, we may have been politely asked to leave.

At the end of October, when I had my first month's evaluation, Sharon asked, "Are you ready to try using the telephone?"

My answer "Not especially," caught her by surprise and she said, "I thought that you would be anxious to try."

Things had been moving along so rapidly and just like the closed captioning on my TV, I wanted to save the telephone for later. But Myron, who was weary of making and taking my calls, urged me to do so. We followed Sharon into her office.

She hooked the telephone adapter, that she had been keeping, into one telephone. She then called me from a second telephone. I picked up my receiver, said, "Hold the line," plugged the adapter into my processor and said, "Hello."

Me and Tanya

I heard her clearly. I really didn't know, though, if I was hearing her over the telephone or if I was hearing her speak from across the room. That evening, when I got a call from my little crafter friend, Tanya, I found out that I had, indeed, heard Sharon "over the telephone." Tanya was calling me from a distance of 300 miles.

When I first met Tanya, she was a little girl of only three who came to the craft sales with her mom and dad. What drew us together, initially, were my doll clothes but even after she grew out of playing with Barbie, we remained friends. When I could no longer hear her, she began to bring a notebook and pen so we could still communicate. We were together so much and we had such a marked resemblance that we were often asked if we were mother and daughter.

Those years went by fast and like all little girls have to do, Tanya grew up and went off to college. She wrote to me often and now she was calling me from her dorm at North Dakota State in Grand Forks, N.D.

She had called Myron earlier in the week and he had told her that I might be using the phone that day. She said she would call then, a secret that he had kept from me.

Me and brother, Alvin after my "Hook-up"

I was hesitant at taking that first call, believe me. But I was able to hear her so well that it was like she was in the same room with me. Then, all of a sudden, I couldn't hear her—my battery had gone dead. Myron finished the call for me.

I was no longer afraid to call after that. My brother, Alvin, was the first to hear from me. I had a hard time convincing him that it really was me. I learned later that when I hung up, he called one friend and relative after another and said, "Guess who I just talked with."

I am ever so thankful that I chose him to call first as a few days before Christmas, I received an unexpected call with the news that he had passed away.

IN THE GARDEN

The call came early in the morning from my brother, Herbert. It was one call that I wished I wasn't hearing right. Unfortunately, I heard every word loud and clear. On the day after Christmas we journeyed once more to Pelican Rapids for his funeral.

It was extremely hard for his brothers, his sister Eleanor, and me to say "Good-bye" to him. He had been the hub of our family. He was the one who, even though he had experienced many rough spots in his life, was able to lift the spirits of others when they were down. To see the outpouring of love and concern by the townspeople was almost more than we could bear.

Just as it had been at Mama's funeral, the church was filled. I had regained my composure somewhat by the time the service began but I lost it completely again when I heard the first strains of "In the Garden" being sung by Robert Kohler, a friend of Alvins.

For days prior to the funeral, the refrain, "He walks with me and he talks with me," had been one of the songs that had been in my heart. I had not connected it to the song "In the Garden" that was now being sung. When he began to sing, "I come to the garden alone..." I let go of all my pent-up emotions. I cried in sadness and I cried in joy that I was able to hear such a beautiful song.

I come to the garden alone
While the dew is still on the roses
And the voice I hear, falling on my ear;
The Son of God discloses.

He speaks and the sound of his voice
Is so sweet the birds hush their singing,
And the melody that he gave to me
Within my heart is ringing.

I'd stay in the garden with him
Tho' the night around me be falling,
But he bids me go; through the voice of woe
His voice to me is calling.

C. Austin Miles

The scene in the basement, where everyone gathered after the funeral, was reminiscent of Mama's funeral but with one big difference. I was able to hear anyone who spoke to me. Because Alvin had spread the wonderful news from one end of Pelican Rapids to the other that his sister could hear again, his funeral became a time for rejoicing.

PART TEN

RECOLLECTIONS-
REFLECTIONS-RESURRECTION

It is my wish that my story, written from the heart, may also become your story. Never, ever, give up hope!

It is good to have an end to journey towards; but it is the journey that matters, in the end.

Ursula K. LeGuin

Before I come to the end of my writing of *Journey Out of Silence,* I want to share with you some very special events that occurred after my hearing was restored. I also want to do some reflecting and tell you how the cochlear implant resurrected me, allowing me to, once again, do the things I couldn't do when I was deaf and the courage and confidence to try new ventures.

One day, not long after I had begun to use the telephone, I was at my sewing machine, diligently sewing one Barbie fashion after another. I looked up to find Scott, some CDs in his hand, standing watching me. Except as an occasional gift for the boys, a CD was of little interest to me so I wondered why he wanted to show them to me. Well, he wasn't going to just show them to me, he was going to play them. He thought it was time for Mom to hear some "real" music.

He laid the CDs down on my sewing machine, said, "I'll be right back," and left. He came back carrying Myron's portable stereo (boom box). He plugged it in, placed one of the CDs in the compartment, looked at me and just as Sharon had when I was "hooked up," he asked me, "Are you ready?"

I wasn't sure if I was or not. I just raised my eyebrows and shrugged my shoulders. He flipped some switches. I sat back in my chair and waited. When I heard Johnny Cash singing, "Don't Take Your Guns to Town," my thought was *Oh, Boy!* The tears didn't just blur my vision that time, they overflowed. With Scott standing by, grinning from ear to ear, I cried like a baby.

I didn't get any more sewing done that day. I spent the next several hours getting reacquainted with Johnny. There were two volumes, one with 23 songs and another with 29 songs. I listened nonstop to both and I replayed some of my favorites over and over.

On and on he sang, each song becoming more resonant than the last. I heard the accompanying music like I had never heard before. The mariachi horns of "Ring of Fire" was sheer delight and I could once more see the train as he played his harmonica rendition of "The Orange Blossom Special" as it came rolling down the track. I heard lyrics that I had never before been able to understand not even after the previous surgeries that gave me an improvement in my hearing. I discovered that he wasn't going to Florida and California to get some bad news! He was going there to have some fun—to get some sand in his shoes.

There was still more to come. Scott had something else up his sleeve. He heard that Johnny Cash was coming to Orchestra Hall in December for a Christmas concert and he ordered tickets for Myron, himself and me. Certainly I would attend. I wasn't about to disappoint either Myron or Scott. I figured I had enough reserved power in my processor to enable me to at least know that it was music.

Santa's visit—1996
Jeffery, Santa, Chelsea, Jacob

The concert began with Johnny Cash and June Carter Cash singing the traditional Christmas carols. I turned the volume down to half. The sounds came through as vibrant as the rising of the sun on a cloudless summer day.

Justin

Then Johnny Cash went solo. He put on his trademark long black coat and came up to the microphone. In his strong, bass voice, he said, "Hello, I'm Johnny Cash."

I erupted along with the rest of the audience. I couldn't believe what I had just heard. It was truly a marvelous evening.

I knew, then, what I wanted for Christmas. I asked Santa to bring me my own personal cassette player and a supply of Christmas carols and country western CDs.

If Christmas had not been overshadowed by the sudden death of my brother, Alvin, it truly would have been my happiest ever. It was the traditional Christmas that our family shared but with something added. My angel, this time dressed as Santa, unexpectedly came over from McDonald's earlier in the week. He consented to returning on Christmas morning when all the grandchildren were there.

I was every bit as excited as they were when he walked in. How phenomenal it all was. In all my 59 years, he had never before come to visit me.

Our third grandson, Justin Michael, was born in the spring, on April 21. Jeffery, Jacob, and Chelsea had all been sleeping soundly when Myron and I first visited them shortly after their births so I figured Justin would be asleep, too. He fooled me!

He had a tummy ache and was crying lustily. The nurse told me to sit in the rocking chair and she placed little Justin in my arms. I didn't try to get him to stop crying. It had been too long since I had heard a newborn baby cry. I sat rocking and listening. There would be plenty of "hush" time in the months to come.

There is yet a third event I wish to share with you. During the winter my sister, Eleanor, made the decision to have the cochlear implant evaluation. I was with her that day in April. I wasn't nervous then and I don't think she was either. She passed the tests and her surgery was scheduled for June.

That's when I began to worry. This was the third time that she would attempt to regain her hearing. The previous stapes mobilization had been unsuccessful and a stapedectomy would not have helped her.

What, if now, something went wrong during surgery or worse yet, she wouldn't be able to hear when she came for her "hook-up?" Would she blame me? Would I ever be able to face her?

I stumbled through the day of her surgery. It went well and she returned home to wait for her hook-up date. I wasn't faring so well and Sharon Smith sensed my dilemma. She suggested that I have a visit with Dr. Robiner, the psychologist I had visited with on my first day of my cochlear implant evaluation.

Three days before Eleanor was to come, we sat down to talk. I walked out of his office a whole lot healthier mentally than when I had walked in.

Eleanor's hook-up was successful. Today she, too, is enjoying the wonders of the sounds that surround her.

Me and Eleanor

I am neither a theologian nor a Doctor of Medicine so I am not going to delve too deeply into the "Whys" or "Hows" of my successful cochlear implant. It has been interesting, though, to hear what others have had to say. Their explanations range from "It's a miracle," to "It was your time." That alone has two versions. One is that it was the right time in my personal life; the other is that it was the right time scientifically.

Some say that my success is due to the fact that my memory of sounds is so vivid and some say it's because I wanted to hear so badly. Some say it was because so many were praying for me; others say it was simply that God answered my prayers.

I am not a philosopher but this is how I think it happened. I think it was God's plan for me just as he says in Isaiah 37:26:

"Have you not heard that I determined it long ago? I planned from days of old what now I bring to pass."

I believe that all of what I was told by others had to "come together" before it could happen.

235

Yes, I do believe it was a miracle, a most wonderful and amazing occurrence. It was the right time for me both personally and scientifically. It would not have had as great an impact on my life ten years ago and neither would I have achieved as great a success then.

I do believe God heard me when I told him that I wanted to hear Jeffery and Jacob's voices and that I wanted them to be able to talk to their grandma. And, without a doubt, I believe it was the power of so many praying for me that brought it to pass. How could he turn a deaf ear to so many?

I believe, too, that the answer to "Why" is also found in the Bible in Proverbs 19:21.

"Many are the plans in the mind of a man, but it is the purpose of the Lord that will be established."

When Sharon flipped the switch on my processor and I heard Myron's voice as I remembered it to be, I knew that I had received a special gift. I knew immediately what I wanted to do with it. In the hopes that others who are living in silence might be helped, I wanted to tell my story and I wanted to do something to directly benefit the University of Minnesota Hospital. I didn't have to wait long to get started.

I wrote my story and it was published in several newspapers and Lions 5M International newsletters. Then I had the opportunity to tell my story in person when I was invited to speak at a Lions 5M Convention and at Trinity Lutheran Church in Detroit Lakes, Minn.

A few weeks later, I became a subject, working in the Cochlear Implant Research Laboratory at the Clinic. That opened up yet another opportunity and I had several hours of free time between my morning and afternoon research sessions. I looked into volunteering.

I attended an orientation and completed the necessary requirements of a volunteer. Then it was time for placement. Naturally, when I saw the Audiology Department listed in the volunteer manual, that was my first choice. Only the manual was outdated and the clinic no longer used the services of volunteers.

I was, however, told that something would be worked out but that it would take awhile. That "awhile" turned into weeks and then months. I grew increasingly restless. Finally, I thought *This isn't where God wants me to be.*

I revisited the Volunteer Office. It was undergoing reorganization and Cheryl, the coordinator at the time, was busy. I only had time to tell her that I was interested in becoming involved with the Ladies' Auxiliary.

Just then Louise Rosendahl came walking down the hallway. I was introduced to her as "Just the lady that you need to speak to."

Louise asked me two questions, "Do you like children?" and "Do you like to read?"

I answered, "I sure do!"

She replied, "Come along. I have the perfect spot for you."

She signed me up as a reader in Project Read. I began my assignment the following Monday. I read in the playroom of the Pediatrics Clinic to little patients and visitors while they wait to see their doctor.

What a blessing it is to be able to hear not only the voices of the children as they ask me questions about the stories but also my own voice. I find the adage, "The more you give, the more you receive," to be so true. For when I see the smiles and get the hugs and "Thank yous" from both children and parents when I pack to leave, I feel that *I* am on the receiving end.

One day I turned around and heard a little girl who had followed me to the elevators ask me in a sad little voice, "Do you have to go?" I knew then that, indeed, Louise had placed me in the perfect spot and that it is part of God's purpose for having restored my hearing. Writing *Journey Out of Silence* was also in his plans and he isn't finished with me yet.

It is my wish that my story may be your story and that you or someone you love will take the journey out of silence.

Hope—that bubbling ingredient in life which is like carbonation in a drink, giving it zest, keeping it in motion, always pushing it up.

De Pree

Girls in Research
Lynn, Me, Gail, Tanya

In the research laboratory
Me and Tanya

*Back row: Sharon, Scott, Chelsea, Kenny, Janine,
Chuck, Jeffery, Myron with Jacob, me with Justin, Dave, Allison*

Timothy Tingelstad, Elisa and Katelyn

READING IN THE PEDIATRIC CLINIC

Nina and me

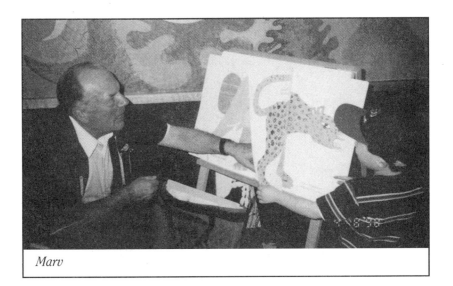

Marv

Children that I read to in Project Read

Me and Dr. Lawrence R. Boies, Jr.

Classmates: Ardy, me, and Ardis

Classmates in the Park in Pelican Rapids
Avis, me, Ardis, Virgie

Me after our house in Pelican Rapids was torn down

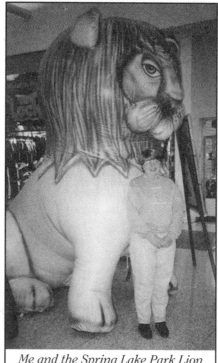

Me and the Spring Lake Park Lion

The Pearson Family today
Back row (left to right): Rob, Tom, Jeanne, Ian, Ann,
Marion, Martha

1997 Cochlear Implant Picnic
Jim Butzer in foreground; first University of Minnesota Implant
Recipient

Myron, me holding Brandon (baptism) and Pastor Howard Shane

Catherine Irving and me after her "hook-up"

Me and classmate Betty at Detroit Lakes Trinity Lutheran Church brunch

AFTERWORD

Cochlear implants have evolved from the single channel devices of 1986 which provided the user with the ability to hear loud and soft and fast or slow speech, to the multiple channel devices of today which have the potential to provide actual speech understanding.

The cochlear implant worn by Dora Weber is the Nucleus 22-Channel cochlear implant. There are several other manufacturers of cochlear implants worldwide, each offering a slightly different benefit and/or limitation. All manufacturers of cochlear implants are required to enter an arduous process of obtaining FDA approval before their devices can be marketed in the United States.

Typically, a limited number of centers are first selected and approved by the FDA to serve as "investigative centers." After the manufacturer collects enough data from these limited number of centers, the FDA approves a larger number of centers to be included in the study. Finally, after enough data has been collected and the manufacturer can prove that the device is safe and effective, FDA approval is applied for and usually received. The whole process can take years.

At the time Dora underwent evaluation for a cochlear implant, there was only one FDA-approved cochlear implant (the Nucleus 22) and one investigative cochlear implant (the Clarion) available through our clinic. By the time Dora received her Nucleus 22-Channel cochlear implant, Clarion had received FDA approval and a third implant, the Med-El Combi 40+ had entered investigational status in the United States.

Technological advances in cochlear implants over the last 12 years seem slow compared with the speed with which they are being both introduced and improved in the past three years. Improvements have led to better speech understanding for the recipients, a loosening of the criteria required for candidacy for the procedure and ultimately a greater number of people receiving implants.

After reading Dora's story, the reader may naturally have many questions. How deaf does a person have to be in order to receive a cochlear implant? Does everyone do as well as Dora? Is it always successful? Have there been any failures? What other hospitals are providing cochlear implants? How much does it cost? Which insurance companies will pay for it? How does an implant recipient take advantage of technological improvements? And finally, how does it work? Dora has asked me to address these questions.

Cochlear implants are designed for individuals who do not receive any benefit from hearing aids in either ear. This is determined by extensive speech understanding testing conducted using the individual's hearing aids. If the individual receives a score below a certain point, they may be a candidate; if they score above a certain level, they are not a candidate. The results of speech perception testing are combined with results from psychological testing, an interview with the cochlear implant surgeon, CT scans and balance testing.

The best candidates are those adults who lost their hearing after learning to talk (post-lingually deafened), children younger than five who lost their hearing before learning to talk (pre-lingually deafened) or post-lingually deafened children of any age. Cochlear implants have also been approved for pre-lingually deafened adults; however, the degree of perceived and measurable benefit tends to be minimal.

There is not any clear-cut way to predict how well a person will do with a cochlear implant. There are those who do not hear as well as Dora does with her cochlear implant just as there are those who hear better. Prediction is impossible, yet there seems to be some evidence that individuals who have been deaf a shorter period of time may show more measurable benefit. Positive attitude and motivation, as in Dora's case, can certainly help carry the individual even further.

Success should be measured in the eye (or ear) of the recipient. While post-operative testing may show identical scores for two individuals, their perceived degree of benefit (or success) may be quite different. Some people measure their degree of benefit in terms of simply being able to hear sound. Others set standards for having conversations, listening to music or using the telephone. Since only about 50 percent of the recipients can use the phone or appreciate music, many fall short of those expectations and may not consider the cochlear implant a complete success.

Cochlear implants can and have failed. This is one of the risks discussed with each patient pre-operatively. There have been five failures in our clinic and a reported rate of three percent world wide. A failed cochlear implant can be removed and replaced with a new one.

Costs for a cochlear implant vary from center to center and state to state. The device alone can cost in the neighborhood of $20,000 with the surgery and follow-up care and training for the first year making up the rest of the cost. Across the nation, costs for the first year may range from $30,000 to over $50,000.

Most states have at least one center which offers cochlear implants. While most insurance companies in Minnesota finally cover the procedure, the majority do so at an abysmally low rate causing most cochlear implant procedures to be money-losing ventures. Most small private practices cannot swallow this loss and so implant centers tend to be found in larger practices or at university hospitals which can supposedly afford these losses. The reader is encouraged to contact the manufacturers of the devices to find the locations of centers and is referred to the last page of this afterword for addresses and phone numbers of those manufacturers.

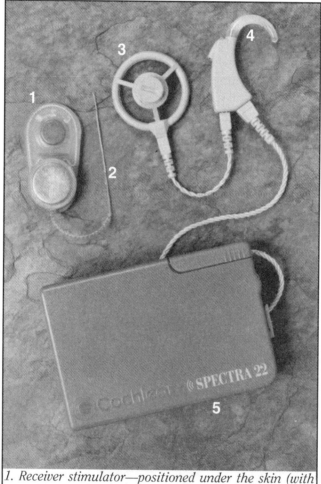

1. Receiver stimulator—positioned under the skin (with magnet) 2. Electrode array—consists of 22 electrodes inserted into cochlea 3. Transmitting coil (with magnet) 4. microphone 5. speech processor

In order to understand how a cochlear implant functions, one must become familiar with all of the components first. All cochlear implants have both external and internal components. The internal components are usually comprised of an electrode array which is inserted by the surgeon into the cochlea (the inner ear). The electrode array is attached to a receiver and an adjacent magnet. The receiver and magnet are placed in an area of bone behind the ear which has been shelled out to hold the receiver. Skin and muscle are sewn over the device and it becomes hidden (although palpable) once the hair grows back. The external components are typically comprised of a speech processor the size of a pack of cards, which may be worn on the belt, in a shirt pocket or in the shirt. Attached to the speech processor is a thin wire which extends up to the head and

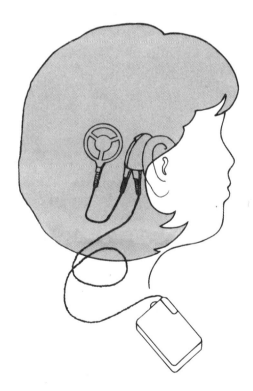

attaches to the transmitter. In some cases, the transmitter and microphone are one piece (e.g. the Clarion); in other cases, as in Dora's Nucleus 22, they are two pieces—the transmitter worn on the scalp and the microphone worn over the ear like a behind-the-ear hearing aid.

Sound is picked up by the microphone and transmitted down the thin wire to the speech processor. The speech processor analyzes and digitizes the information and sends it back up the wire to the transmitter, which sends the information by radio frequency (no, you cannot pick up any radio stations or open any garage doors with this!) to the receiver inside the head. The receiver transduces the information into electrical signals and sends the information down the electrode array, instructing which electrode should stimulate the hearing nerve. The nerve sends the information to the brain which understands the stimulation as meaningful sound.

Technological advances in existing cochlear implants have, for the most part, involved miniaturization of the speech processors and improved speech processing strategies. These advances have involved simply upgrading computer software and have not required undergoing surgery once again. However, there have been some hardware changes over the years which have served to improve the devices. Taking advantage of these hardware changes would involve undergoing explantation and reimplantation of a new device.

The future of cochlear implants looks exciting as manufacturers plan to reduce the size of the speech processor to an ear-level speech processor and some day make all of the components completely implantable.

Dora Weber was the 98th person to receive a cochlear implant at what is now Fairview-University Medical Center. She came in at a time when a difficult decision had to be made regarding which implant system to choose. She chose the Clarion; however, due to difficulties during surgery, the choice of a Nucleus was made for her. With the Nucleus-22, she has achieved very good speech recognition abilities, can engage in conversations over the telephone and can appreciate music. Her joy and enthusiasm at being able to hear again is infectious, has made working with her a pleasure, and she has motivated other deaf individuals to embark on similar journeys out of silence.

> Sharon Smith, M.S. CCC-A
> Coordinator, Cochlear Implant Program
> Fairview-University Medical Center

To obtain more information related to Nucleus devices:

> Cochlear Corporation
> 61 Inverness Drive E. Suite 200
> Englewood, CO 80112-9726
> (800) 523-5798

To obtain more information related to Clarion devices:

> Advanced Bionics Corporation
> 12740 San Fernando Road
> Sylmar, CA 91342
> (800) 678-2575
> TDD: (800) 678-3575

For information regarding Fairview-University Medical Center's Cochlear Implant Program, contact:

> Sharon Smith, M.S. CCC-A
> Coordinator, Cochlear Implant Program
> Box 396 FUMC
> Harvard Street at East River Road
> Minneapolis, MN 55455
> (800) 688-5252 ext. 51689

GLOSSARY

George L. Adams, M.D.
Professor and Head,
Department of Otolaryngology-Head & Neck Surgery
University of Minnesota

OTOSCLEROSIS—An underlying hereditary disease that is dominant in character, that is, the majority of people who carry the gene will at some point, develop the disease. However, because it is an incomplete dominance, not everyone who carries the gene will develop the disease. It appears to be more common in women. It usually develops in the early 20s and has been known to be more progressive during pregnancy. The disease process was first thought to be limited to the stapes (the third bone in the chain that attaches to the inner ear), but was later found to involve other areas of the bone around the inner ear. The term otosclerosis is actually misleading; sclerosis tends to mean firm or hardness. In fact, a better term would be otospongiosis, as the bone that becomes involved actually becomes soft. The disease process often burns itself out by middle age leaving the individual with a conductive hearing loss, that is, hearing loss due to something in the middle ear, yet a perfectly functioning nerve associated with the inner ear and brain.

TINNITUS—This term means the rushing or ringing sound emanating from the inner ear. It is usually a subjective rather than an objective finding, that is, in almost all cases, the individual with the problem hears the sound, but no one else can. It is often associated with a high tone nerve loss.

FENESTRATION—This, of course, means creating a window or fenestre. What was done originally prior to stapes surgery was that a window was created over the horizontal canal. Again, there was fear that if one were to remove or damage the stapes, opening the middle ear to the inner ear, the patient would go immediately deaf. Thus, a substitute plan was to create an opening into the inner ear to the horizontal semi-circular canal, part of the vestibular system. This would allow transmission of the sound to the underlying fluid, which would then transmit the sound to the nerves of the inner ear. This technique gave way to the more modern technique of removing the stapes referred to as stapedectomy. Primarily physicians in New York, the best known of whom was Julius Lempert, performed it.

STAPEDECTOMY—There was originally a great fear that if the surgeon removed the bone that connected the middle ear chain of bones to the inner ear, the patient would invariably go deaf. Dr. John Shae, now in Memphis, was the first to actually show that this bone could safely be removed, a patch of vein placed over the new opening and an artificial or metal bone inserted.

STAPES MOBILIZATION—Prior to the stapedectomy, doctors in New York simply fractured and mobilized the stapes bone but did not remove it. Of course, the problem here was that the bone would reaffix in time, usually within a few years.

PROMONTORY STIMULATION—If there was no eardrum present and only an exposed middle ear, examination would reveal a round eminence or promontory. This represents the basal turn, or lowest turn, of the cochlea. It is the most accessible area of the cochlea as the rest of it is buried further in the head in dense bone. Thus, by placing an electrode or electrical stimulation directly on the bone overlying the basal turn of the cochlea and applying an electrical current, stimulation can occur. If the patient having this test feels only an electric shock and pain, then it is unlikely that a cochlear implant would be effective. On the other hand, if, by stimulating the basal turn with a low-dose of electricity, the patient actually hears a sound or something that he or she interprets as a sound, then it is thought that the cochlear implant would be more effective.

About the Author

Dora and Myron

Dora Weber, who made a long and arduous journey out of silence, shares her experiences in an effort to encourage those who are hearing impaired and to increase the sensitivity of those who are not. Her compelling story tells about her world as a hearing person, through the hard times when she gradually lost her hearing, and to the happy ending which awaited her.

During her years of silence, Dora built up a thriving business of sewing doll clothes. In order to have more time to serve as an advocate for the cochlear implant program, she is giving up her business after 35 years.

As a subject, Dora participates in the research of the cochlear implant. She encourages prospective cochlear implant candidates and serves as interim co-ordinator of Cochlear Implant Club International Chapter of Minnesota.

Dora also does volunteer work for the University of Minnesota Health System Auxiliary. She is a reader for the Project Read Program and does medical sewing for the Fairview University Medical Center.

Journey Out of Silence is also the story of Dora's family who supported her as she made her way back to the hearing world. She has been married to Myron Weber for over 35 years and they are the parents of four sons. At present, they have five grandchildren, Jeffery, Justin, Jacob, Chelsea and Brandon and are anticipating the arrival of a sixth.

Dora and Myron are members of Prince of Peace Lutheran Church, Spring Lake Park, Minn. where Myron serves as secretary of the Church Council.

Do You Hear What I Hear?

Do you hear what I hear
  Do you hear what I hear
    Wintry winds that blow
      And the crunch of footsteps in the snow

Do you hear what I hear
  Do you hear what I hear
    Christmas in the air
      And bells that are ringing everywhere

Do you hear what I hear
  Do you hear what I hear
    Voices of the children ring
      Telling Santa what to bring

Do you hear what I hear
  Do you hear what I hear
    Carols being sung
      Of Silent Night and Holy Night
        And Bethlehem, the little town
          When kings and shepherds traveled far
            'till the Christ child was found

Do you hear what I hear
  I can hear what you hear
    My Christmas wish is that all may hear
      "Merry Christmas and Happy New Year"